FAITH CLINIC

VOLUME XXI

-ABANDONMENT EDITION-

They Didn't Leave God, They Left You

DR. PATRICIA S. TANNER

©Copyright 2026

IBG Publications, Inc.

DR. PATRICIA S. TANNER

Published by I.B.G. Publications, Inc., a Power to Wealth Company

Web address: www.ibgpublications.com

admin@ibgpublications.com / 904-419-9810

Copyright, 2026 by Patricia S. Tanner

IBG Publications, Inc., Jacksonville, FL

ISBN: 978-1-971850-05-4

Tanner, Patricia S.
Faith Clinic, Volume XXI Abandonment Edition-They Didn't Leave
God, They Left You

Printed in the United States of America.

DEDICATION

To the ones who loved deeply and were left.

To those who stayed loyal, served faithfully, trusted openly, and found themselves wounded in sacred spaces.

This book is dedicated to every heart that felt abandoned by people and almost walked away from God because of it.

May you heal without becoming hard.
May you trust again without losing wisdom.
And may you discover that even when people failed you, God never did.

With compassion,

DR. PATRICIA S. TANNER
The Faith Doctor

TABLE OF CONTENTS

📖 WELCOME TO THE CLINIC

Patient Name: You

Chief Complaint: " I'm not mad… I'm just tired of people leaving."

Secondary Symptoms:

- Hyper-independence with a praise playlist
- Trust issues disguised as discernment
- Emotional detachment marketed as "boundaries"
- Smiling at church while secretly planning your exit strategy from relationships

Initial Assessment:

Patient has confused abandonment with spiritual failure and is attempting to heal relational trauma using Bible verses meant for persecution, not neglect.

Clinical Note:
This will require honesty, not hustle.

📖 FAITH CLINIC INTAKE FORM

WELCOME TO THE FAITH CLINIC

Before we begin, please note:

- ✓ This is **not** a safe space for pretending you're fine. This is a healing space for people who learned how to survive abandonment and called it strength.
- ✓ If you're looking for quick forgiveness tips, shallow encouragement, or a scripture to slap on unresolved pain, this clinic may cause discomfort, clarity, and emotional detox.
- ✓ Please complete this intake form honestly. No one is grading you.

  But your healing depends on your answers.

📋 PATIENT INFORMATION

Patient Name: ___________________________________

(If you put "It doesn't matter," please circle why.)

Age: ___________

***Spiritual Background* (check all that apply):**

☐ Raised in church

☐ Found God later

☐ Took a break because people ruined it

☐ Still believes, just tired

☐ " It's complicated"

***Current Spiritual Status*:**
☐ Actively serving
☐ Attending but guarded

☐ Spiritually present, emotionally checked out
☐ Praying quietly and trusting nobody
☐ Showing up out of habit, not hope

⚕ CHIEF COMPLAINT

(What brings you into the clinic today?)
☐ People keep leaving
☐ I'm tired of being "the strong one"
☐ I don't trust anyone anymore—and I call it discernment
☐ I feel abandoned but don't want to sound ungrateful
☐ I stayed longer than I should have
☐ I don't know how to let people get close anymore
☐ I feel closer to God than people—and that scares me
☐ Other: ____

🧠 SYMPTOM CHECKLIST

(Check all that apply. This is a judgment-free zone. Mostly.)
☐ Hyper-independence ("I'll just do it myself")
☐ Emotional detachment with a Bible verse attached
☐ Apologizing for having needs
☐ Feeling disposable in relationships
☐ Over-explaining to people who already decided to leave
☐ Avoiding confrontation because abandonment feels worse than disrespect
☐ Smiling in public, grieving in private
☐ Loyalty to people who wouldn't choose me back
☐ Leaving first so it hurts less
☐ Calling numbness "peace"

✏ HISTORY OF PRESENT ILLNESS

DR. PATRICIA S. TANNER

(Answer honestly. God already knows.)

1. **Have you ever been left without explanation?**
   ☐ Yes
   ☐ More times than I can count
   ☐ They explained—but it still didn't make sense
2. **Who caused the deepest abandonment wound?**
   ☐ Family
   ☐ Church leadership
   ☐ Friends
   ☐ A romantic relationship
   ☐ A season where everyone disappeared at once
3. **Did anyone ever minimize your pain by saying:**
   ☐ " God removes people for a reason"
   ☐ " You're too sensitive"
   ☐ " Just forgive and move on"
   ☐ " It's just a season"
   ☐ " You shouldn't expect so much from people"

(Please underline the one that still makes your chest tighten.)

☖ COPING MECHANISMS

(How have you been managing the pain?)

☐ Staying busy
☐ Staying distant
☐ Staying silent
☐ Staying loyal past expiration dates
☐ Staying in prayer but avoiding people
☐ Staying guarded and calling it wisdom
☐ Staying numb
☐ Staying strong because no one offered support

📖 SPIRITUAL SIDE EFFECTS OBSERVED

☐ Difficulty trusting God's timing
☐ Difficulty trusting people God sends
☐ Fear that closeness always ends in loss
☐ Confusion between discernment and fear
☐ Avoidance of community
☐ Over-spiritualizing abandonment to avoid grief
☐ Feeling chosen by God but unwanted by people

📝 PATIENT STATEMENT

(Complete the sentence honestly.)
- "The hardest part of being abandoned was not
________________________, it was ______________________."
- "I learned to survive abandonment by
________________________."
- "If I'm honest, I'm afraid that if I let people in again,
________________________."

💀 PRELIMINARY DIAGNOSIS

(To be confirmed through teaching, reflection, and truth exposure.)
☐ Chronic Abandonment Trauma
☐ Emotional Self-Reliance Disorder
☐ Trust Avoidance with Spiritual Justification
☐ Grief Suppression
☐ Relational Guarding Syndrome

Clinical Note:
Patient appears spiritually committed but emotionally exhausted.
Faith remains intact. Trust systems require rehabilitation.

DR. PATRICIA S. TANNER

⚠ IMPORTANT DISCLOSURE

This treatment plan may include:

- Naming what happened instead of spiritualizing it

- Releasing responsibility for people who chose to leave

- Learning the difference between being chosen by God and tolerated by people

- Letting go of loyalty that costs your peace

- Rebuilding trust without abandoning yourself

Side effects may include:

✓ Relief

✓ Tears

✓ Anger you weren't "allowed" to feel

✓ Unexpected laughter

✓ Peace that doesn't require explanation

✒ PATIENT SIGNATURE

By signing below, you acknowledge that healing will require honesty, boundaries, and truth—not just time.

Signature: ________________________________

Date: ____________________

⚠ FAITH CLINIC: EMERGENCY RELAPSE WALLET CARD

◍ FRONT OF CARD
EMERGENCY RELAPSE NOTICE
If you are currently:
- Rewriting the past to excuse someone who left.
- Blaming yourself for someone else's exit.
- Tempted to reach out for closure that will not close anything.
- Romanticizing people who abandoned you.
- Wondering if you were "too much" or "not enough."

STOP.
This is not intuition.
This is abandonment trauma looking for a familiar ache.

◍ BREATH CHECK (Do This First)

Inhale for **4 seconds**
Hold for **4 seconds**
Exhale for **6 seconds**
Repeat until your nervous system remembers you are safe **right now**.
You are not being abandoned in this moment.
You are being triggered by a memory.

🧠 REALITY REMINDER

(Read out loud if possible. Whisper counts.)
- I did not imagine the distance.
- I did not cause someone else's inability to stay.
- Love that requires me to disappear is not love—it is tolerance.
- God did not leave me. People made a choice.

- Closure is not my responsibility. Healing is.

⬡ RELAPSE WARNING SIGNS

(Check all that apply)
- ☐ Urge to explain yourself again
- ☐ Believing silence means rejection
- ☐ Wanting to prove your worth
- ☐ Reopening wounds for temporary comfort
- ☐ Missing the person more than the peace
- ☐ Confusing familiarity with safety

Clinical Note:
Missing someone does not mean you should return.

⚕ DOCTOR'S ORDERS: IMMEDIATE CARE

Instead of reaching out:
- ✓ Journal what you wish they had said
- ✓ Take a walk or change environments
- ✓ Pray without editing your feelings
- ✓ Read one chapter of this book
- ✓ Remind yourself why healing started

Do not contact anyone who left until this urge passes.
Urges are temporary. Damage can be permanent.

❧ HOLY SPIRIT CONSULT

(Short. Honest. No performance.)
"God, I'm triggered—not abandoned.
Help me stay present instead of chasing the past.
Return my peace without reopening the wound.
Amen."

⬤ BACK OF CARD

FINAL TRUTH — READ THIS SLOWLY

- ✓ You were not abandoned because you were unworthy.
- ✓ You were released because not everyone is equipped to walk with you.
- ✓ This ache will pass.
- ✓ Your dignity does not depend on their return.
- ✓ Healing is happening, even when it feels quiet.
- ✓ Fold this card. Keep it close.
  You are not regressing, you are recalibrating.

PERSONAL NOTES

INTRODUCTION

Abandonment: It's Not Church Hurt, It's People Hurt

There is a particular kind of pain that does not come from sin, rebellion, or failure, yet somehow still gets treated as if it did. It is the pain of being left behind without explanation, without closure, and without permission to grieve. It is the kind of pain that does not announce itself loudly but settles quietly into the body, reshaping how you trust, how you attach, and how you interpret silence. For many believers, this pain becomes even more confusing because it happens in spaces where love, commitment, and faith are supposed to be safe.

This book exists because abandonment has been mislabeled for far too long.

What many people call church hurt is often not institutional damage at all. It is relational injury caused by people who did not know how to stay, who did not know how to communicate, or who did not know how to carry responsibility when things became uncomfortable. Churches did not always wound you. People did. And the expectation that you should be spiritually unaffected by that reality has caused more harm than healing.

You did not stop believing in God. You stopped believing that people would remain present when life stopped being easy. That distinction matters, even if no one ever gave you permission to say it out loud.

Abandonment rarely arrives in dramatic fashion. It does not always come with betrayal, confrontation, or obvious wrongdoing. More often, it arrives quietly. It shows up as messages that stop being returned, conversations that never happen, support that fades when you need it most, and relationships that dissolve without warning. You were still showing up while others were slowly stepping away, and when you finally noticed the distance, you were already alone in it.

What makes abandonment especially painful is not only the loss of connection but the way it forces you to interpret yourself. You begin asking questions that feel spiritual but are actually rooted in self-blame. You wonder if you were too much, not enough, or somehow misaligned with God's will. You examine your words, your tone, your growth, and your calling, as if abandonment were evidence of personal failure. And because you are a person of faith, you often turn that examination inward instead of outward, assuming that the responsibility must belong to you.

Well-meaning advice rarely helps. Phrases like "God removes people for a reason" or "It was just a season" sound comforting, but they often bypass grief instead of addressing it. They rush healing before honesty has had a chance to breathe. They teach you to spiritualize pain rather than process it, and they leave you feeling guilty for hurting when you are supposed to be grateful.

This book is not interested in helping you move on quickly. It is interested in helping you heal honestly.

Abandonment does more than wound the heart. It subtly trains the nervous system to expect loss, the mind to anticipate rejection, and the spirit to brace instead of trust. Over time, it reshapes how you show up in relationships. You become more independent than you want to be, more guarded than you admit, and more tired than you allow yourself to acknowledge. You learn how to survive without support and call it strength. You learn how to stay quiet about your needs and call it maturity. You learn how to function while fractured.

None of that means you are broken. It means something real happened to you.

The Faith Clinic was created to address wounds that were never treated, only managed. It does not rush forgiveness, glorify suffering, or reward emotional suppression. It does not hand out scripture as anesthesia for unresolved pain. Instead, it slows the process down long enough to ask the questions that matter. What happened to you? What did you lose? What conclusions did you draw about yourself as a result?

In this clinic, healing begins with truth. Not harsh truth, and not performative spirituality, but steady, grounded clarity. You are not required to minimize what happened to be faithful. You are not disobedient for grieving. You are not weak for admitting that being left changed you.

This book will not encourage bitterness, but it will refuse denial. It will not teach you to distrust everyone, but it will help you rebuild trust without abandoning yourself in the process. It will not tell you that God caused people to leave, but it will show you how God remains present when they do.

Some chapters may feel gentle, while others may feel confrontational. Some pages may bring relief, while others may bring tears. That is not a failure of faith. That is the beginning of healing.

DR. PATRICIA S. TANNER

If you have ever questioned your worth because others did not stay, if you have ever learned to rely on yourself because no one else showed up, and if you have ever confused abandonment with divine disapproval, this book was written with you in mind.

You are not dramatic.
You are not deficient.
You are not behind.
You are human, and something painful happened to you.
Welcome to the Faith Clinic. This time, you do not have to pretend you are fine.

Part 1

THE DIAGNOSIS

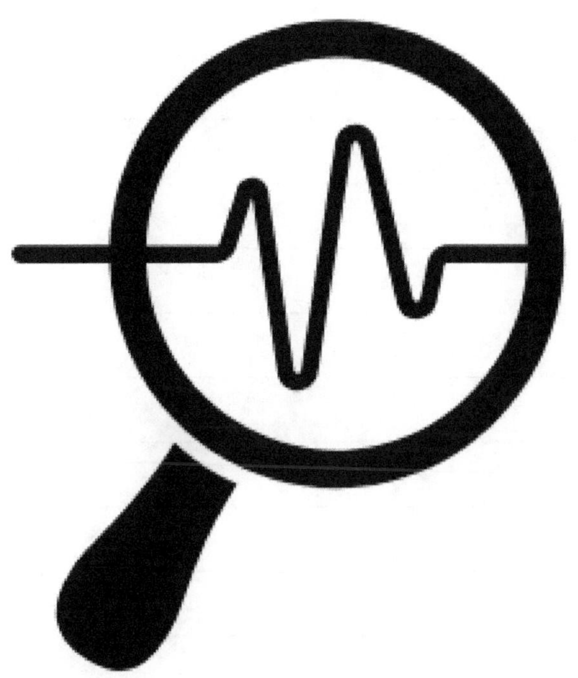

DR. PATRICIA S. TANNER

PERSONAL NOTES

Chapter 1

"If I Was So Anointed, Why Did Everyone Leave?"

SYMPTOM: When Abandonment Starts To Feel Like A Spiritual Failure

There is a particular kind of pain that doesn't just hurt your heart, it interrogates your worth. It doesn't scream; it whispers. It doesn't accuse loudly; it quietly suggests. And the suggestion sounds something like this: *If you were really loved... if you were really called... if you were valuable... people would have stayed.*

This is the symptom most people don't know how to name, so they spiritualize it instead.

You don't just miss the people who left. You start reviewing yourself like a rejected résumé. You replay conversations, tone shifts, unanswered messages, subtle withdrawals. You ask yourself what you did wrong, what you should have done differently, what version of yourself might have been easier to keep. And because you're a believer, you don't stop at self-examination, you turn it into self-indictment.

- ✓ You begin to wonder if your anointing was exaggerated.
- ✓ If your calling was misunderstood.
- ✓ If your faith was louder than your fruit.

And no one around you helps, because the well-meaning advice sounds like this: *"God removes people for a reason."* Which sounds spiritual, until you realize it places the emotional burden back on you to accept pain without processing it.

So instead of grieving abandonment, you spiritualize it. Instead of naming loss, you call it obedience. Instead of admitting it hurt, you say, "I'm fine. God's got me."

And maybe He does, but you're still bleeding.

This symptom shows up quietly. It shows up when you stop expecting consistency from people. When you stop asking questions. When you stop letting yourself need. It shows up when you convince yourself that loneliness is the price of maturity and isolation is a sign of growth. You tell yourself you're just "set apart," when really, you're just tired of being left.

The most dangerous part of this symptom is not the pain; it's the conclusion you draw from it. You start believing that if people don't stay, then something must be wrong with you.

TEACHING: Anointing Does Not Equal Retention

Let's say this clearly, slowly, and without religious padding:
People leaving your life is not evidence that you lack anointing. In many cases, it's evidence that you outgrew their capacity.

Scripture never promises that being called means being kept. In fact, the Bible is brutally honest about the opposite. Those most aligned with God often experienced the highest level of abandonment, not because they failed, but because their presence exposed what others were unwilling to confront. 

Jesus did not lose people because He was unclear. He lost people because He refused to dilute truth for comfort. And yet, we read the story backward when it happens to us. We assume departure equals disapproval. We assume silence equals rejection. We assume loss equals fault. But anointing has always attracted two kinds of responses: devotion and departure. There is no third category.

   ✓ Some people leave because they are offended.

✓ Some leave because they are convicted.
✓ Some leave because your growth confronts their stagnation.
✓ And some leave because they simply lack the emotional or spiritual capacity to walk with you where you're going.
✓ None of those require you to shrink.

The problem is that abandonment rarely comes with explanation. It comes with silence. And silence is fertile ground for lies. Silence allows your mind to fill in gaps with self-blame. Silence invites your insecurity to take the microphone and preach a sermon God never authored. So, this teaching is not here to tell you that abandonment didn't hurt. It hurt deeply. But pain does not get to define truth.

✓ You were not left because you were too much.
✓ You were not left because you lacked value.
✓ You were not left because God changed His mind about you.
✓ You were left because not everyone is assigned to stay.

Anointing attracts access, but it also exposes limits. Some people can admire you from a distance but cannot walk with you up close. Some can benefit from your presence but cannot commit to the responsibility it requires. And when those people leave, it feels personal, but it is positional.

This is where healing begins, not when you understand *why* they left, but when you stop making their leaving a verdict on your worth.

The Faith Clinic does not teach you how to numb pain with scripture. It teaches you how to tell the ***truth*** without drowning in it. And the truth here is this: abandonment is not proof that something is wrong with you. It is often proof that something was no longer aligned.

You don't heal abandonment by convincing yourself it didn't matter.

You heal it by refusing to let it redefine who you are. And until you stop equating people staying with God approving, you will keep questioning your value every time someone walks away.

This chapter is your first diagnosis, not because something is wrong with you, but because something false has been lodged in your thinking. You didn't lose people because you weren't anointed enough. You lost them because not everyone is equipped to stay in rooms where growth is happening.

CLINICAL NOTE (Faith Clinic Assessment)

- ✓ Patient exhibits internalized abandonment narratives masked as humility.
- ✓ Faith is intact. Identity requires recalibration.
- ✓ Treatment will focus on truth exposure, grief permission, and restoring self-trust without bitterness.

💊 FAITH PRESCRIPTION

Reframing Abandonment Without Rewriting Yourself

Prescription Name: Truth Exposure Therapy
Dosage: Daily, especially when self-doubt flares
Duration: Ongoing; do not discontinue when symptoms lessen
Refills: Unlimited, because healing is layered

Instructions for Use:
You are not required to understand why someone left to heal from it. Clarity is helpful, but it is not necessary. The goal of this prescription is not to give you answers, it is to interrupt the false conclusions you've been carrying.

For years, you may have treated abandonment like evidence. Evidence that you were lacking. Evidence that you were misaligned. Evidence that you misunderstood your calling, your worth, or your place. This prescription challenges that narrative, not aggressively, but consistently.

Each time the thought arises, *"If I mattered, they would have stayed,"* you will replace it with this truth:
"Their leaving explains their limits, not my value."
This is not denial. It is discernment without self-harm.

You are instructed to stop reviewing your past through the lens of rejection. Stop analyzing yourself as if you were the problem to be solved. Healing begins when you stop treating abandonment like a character flaw and start recognizing it as a relational fracture that was never meant to be carried alone.

Important Warning:
Do not confuse reflection with rumination. One leads to growth.
The other keeps the wound open.
If this prescription causes discomfort, sadness, or grief—do not discontinue. These are signs the truth is reaching places that survival once protected.

🕊 HOLY SPIRIT CONSULT

A Gentle Interruption To The Voice Of Self-Blame

This consult is not dramatic.
It is quiet.
It is steady.
It sounds less like thunder and more like reassurance.
The Holy Spirit is not asking you to be stronger.
He is asking you to be honest.
He is not pointing out what you did wrong.
He is reminding you of what you forgot.

That you were faithful even when others were inconsistent.
That you stayed open longer than most would have.
That your heart did not fail, you were simply outpaced by people who could not keep up with the weight of real connection.
The Spirit is not offended by your questions.
He is not disappointed by your pain.
He is not surprised by your grief.
And He is gently correcting this belief you've been carrying:
"Being left does not mean being unloved."
You are not behind.
You are not disqualified.
You are not on spiritual probation.
You are healing from something that hurts.
And heaven is not rushing you.

GUIDED PRAYER

(Honest. Unguarded. No performance required.)
"God, I need You to help me separate what happened to me from what I believe about myself. I admit that I've been carrying abandonment like a verdict, like people leaving meant something was wrong with me.
I've replayed moments, blamed myself, and questioned my worth in ways You never asked me to.
I'm tired of turning loss into self-accusation.
I'm tired of spiritualizing pain instead of healing it.
Help me release the need to understand every exit.
Help me stop measuring my value by who stayed.
Help me trust that You were present even when people were absent.
I don't want to be guarded; I want to be whole.
I don't want to be numb; I want to be healed.
I don't want to confuse abandonment with identity anymore.
Teach me how to grieve without blaming myself.
Teach me how to trust without disappearing.
Teach me how to stand in truth without becoming bitter.

*I place my worth back in Your hands, where it always belonged.
Amen."*

📝 JOURNAL REFLECTION PAGE

Answer Slowly. Honesty Over Eloquence.

Take a breath before you write. You are not being evaluated, you
are being invited inward.

1. When people left, what story did I tell myself about why they
    left? (Not the polite answer. The honest one.)

2. How has abandonment shaped the way I show up in
    relationships now? (What do I avoid? What do I control? What
    do I withhold?)

3. What part of my worth did I unknowingly hand over to someone
    who couldn't carry it?

____

____

____

____

____

4. What would it look like to believe that their leaving was about capacity, not my value?

____

____

____

____

____

5. What truth do I need to return to when this wound gets triggered again? (Write it in your own words. Keep it close.)

____

____

____

____

____

____

⚕ CLOSING CLINICAL NOTE

This chapter does not end with closure.
It ends with clarity.
You were not abandoned because you were unworthy.
You were not left because you failed.
You were not forgotten by God while people disappeared.

You were in a season where truth required separation.

And this is only the beginning of learning how to stay with yourself.

PERSONAL NOTES

____

____

____

____

____

____

____

____

____

____

Chapter 2

"God Didn't Ghost You, People Did"

SYMPTOM: When Silence From People Starts To Sound Like Silence From God

One of the most disorienting side effects of abandonment is how easily it distorts your perception of God. It begins subtly, almost imperceptibly. People stop showing up, communication fades, support disappears, and before you realize it, your disappointment with humans has quietly bled into your expectations of God. You do not consciously accuse Him of leaving, but you begin to wonder why He feels quieter than before, slower than expected, or more distant than you remember.

This symptom does not announce itself as unbelief. It disguises itself as confusion.

You pray, but the prayers feel unanswered. You read scripture, but the words feel less alive. You worship, but something inside you stays guarded, as if you are bracing for another letdown. You tell yourself God is teaching you patience, but deep down you are asking a different question altogether: *If God is present, why does everything feel so empty?*

What makes this symptom especially painful is that it comes wrapped in spiritual language. You are told that God is silent because He is refining you, testing you, or calling you deeper. While there may be truth in those ideas, they often bypass the more immediate reality, you are grieving human absence, not divine withdrawal. But because no one taught you how to separate the two, your heart blends them together.

When people leave without explanation, silence becomes threatening. It no longer feels neutral. It feels loaded. Silence feels like rejection, like punishment, like proof that something has gone wrong. So when God does not respond in the way you expect, your nervous system reacts before your theology has time to catch up. You begin to assume that His quietness carries the same meaning as theirs.

This is how abandonment trauma works. It teaches you to interpret absence as abandonment and quietness as disapproval. It convinces you that if God loved you enough, He would intervene more quickly, speak more clearly, or fix the pain before it settled so deeply. And when He does not, you quietly pull back, not in rebellion, but in self-protection.

The symptom is not that you stop believing in God. The symptom is that you stop expecting closeness.

You remain faithful, but you become cautious. You still pray, but you no longer pour your heart out. You show up spiritually, but emotionally you hold back, because somewhere along the way you learned that presence is temporary and attachment is risky. What began as disappointment with people slowly becomes distance from God, not because He left, but because silence now feels unsafe.

TEACHING: Silence Is Not Abandonment, And Absence Is Not God's Language

This teaching requires careful distinction, because confusion here can quietly reshape your faith for years if left unaddressed. God does not communicate abandonment through silence.

People do.

Human silence often carries avoidance, discomfort, or emotional immaturity. It is frequently used to escape responsibility, difficult conversations, or relational accountability. When people go quiet, it is often because they do not know how to show up honestly. God's silence, however, is not avoidance. It is not withdrawal. It is not rejection. And it is never passive-aggressive.

Scripture consistently shows us that God's presence is not dependent on noise. He is present in the stillness as much as He is in the storm. But abandonment teaches the heart to fear quiet spaces, because quiet once meant loss. When people disappeared without explanation, silence became associated with danger. So, when God does not respond immediately, the wound interprets it as abandonment rather than invitation.

This is where faith and trauma collide.

God's quietness is often an invitation to trust, not a signal to retreat. It is a space for growth, not punishment. Yet when your nervous system has been trained by abandonment, it reacts to God's quietness the same way it reacted to people leaving. It tightens. It braces. It pulls away before it can be hurt again.

The truth is this: God has not ghosted you. He does not disappear without intention, explanation, or care. Even when He feels quiet, He remains attentive. Even when He does not intervene the way you expect, He does not withdraw His presence. What feels like distance is often the overlap of grief and unmet expectations, not divine absence.

Jesus Himself experienced human abandonment while remaining fully held by God. The disciples scattered. The crowd disappeared. Support vanished at the moment of greatest need. Yet even in that isolation, God's presence did not waver. The abandonment came from people, not from heaven.

Understanding this distinction is essential for healing. Until you separate human absence from divine presence, you will continue guarding yourself from God in moments when you need Him most. You will interpret quiet seasons as rejection and a mistake waiting to be forgotten.

- ✓ God's silence is not punishment.
- ✓ God's quietness is not abandonment.
- ✓ God's presence is not measured by constant reassurance.
- ✓ He is not distant because people left.
- ✓ He is not quiet because you failed.
- ✓ He is not withholding because you are unworthy.

What feels like silence is often God refusing to compete with the noise of grief, shame, and self-blame that abandonment created. Healing begins when you stop assigning human behavior to a divine character and allow God to be who He has always been, faithful, steady, and near, even when He is not loud.

CLINICAL NOTE (Faith Clinic Assessment)

Patient exhibits emotional transference, projecting human abandonment onto divine relationships. Faith remains present; trust has been disrupted by unresolved grief. Treatment will focus on distinguishing God's presence from human behavior and restoring relational safety with God.

🔖 FAITH PRESCRIPTION

Separating God's Presence from People's Absence

Prescription Name: Presence Reorientation Therapy
Dosage: Daily, especially during quiet or triggering seasons
Duration: Ongoing; do not discontinue during silence
Refills: Unlimited

Instructions for Use:
This prescription is not meant to make God louder. It is meant to make your interpretation clearer. Abandonment teaches the heart to associate silence with loss. Over time, your mind learned to fill quiet spaces with fear, self-blame, and expectation of rejection. This prescription interrupts that reflex by retraining your understanding of what silence means, especially in your relationship with God.

When people go quiet, they often leave emotionally, relationally, or permanently. God does not do that. His silence does not signal disinterest, withdrawal, or punishment. It often signals steadiness, an invitation to remain present without being reassured every moment.

Each time you catch yourself thinking, *"God feels distant,"* you are instructed to ask a different question: ***"What am I grieving right now?"***
Because unresolved grief will always speak louder than truth.

This prescription asks you to stop demanding constant emotional feedback from God as proof of His presence. Faith is not sustained by constant sensation. It is sustained by trust built over time. Silence is not abandonment; it is often the space where trust matures.

Important Warning:
Do not confuse God's quietness with indifference. One is an invitation. The other is a wound talking.

🕊 HOLY SPIRIT CONSULT

Restoring Safety in Quiet Spaces

The Holy Spirit is not offended by your hesitation.
He understands why silence feels threatening to you.
He knows that silence once meant being forgotten.
He knows that unanswered messages trained you to expect loss.
He knows that people disappeared when you needed clarity the most.
And He is gently saying this: "I am not like them."
The Spirit is not asking you to force closeness. He is inviting you to remain open without bracing for impact. He is teaching you that stillness with God is not something to survive, it is something to rest in.

You do not have to perform to keep God's attention.
You do not have to fill the quiet to remain loved.
You do not have to earn reassurance to be held.
The Holy Spirit is restoring a sense of safety that abandonment disrupted. He is teaching your heart that presence does not always announce itself, but it never disappears.

🙏 GUIDED PRAYER

(Slow. Honest. Unedited.)
"God, I admit that silence makes me uncomfortable. Not because I doubt You, but because I've been left before. I confess that when people disappeared, I learned to associate quiet with loss.

So, when You feel quiet, my heart assumes distance, even when my faith knows better. Help me separate what people did from who You are. Help me stop projecting human absence onto divine presence. Help me trust You in the quiet without filling it with fear.

I don't want to guard myself from You. I don't want to pull back just because I'm afraid of being disappointed again. Teach me how to rest in Your presence without needing constant reassurance. Teach me how to stay open even when You are not loud. Teach me how to trust that You are near, even when my feelings say otherwise.
I choose to believe that You did not leave me.
I choose to believe that silence is not rejection.
I choose to stay. Amen."

📝 JOURNAL REFLECTION PAGE

Let the Silence Speak: Without Letting It Accuse You
Answer these slowly. There is no rush here.

1. When God feels quiet, what do I usually assume it means? (Be honest, this reveals the wound, not your faith.)

____

____

____

____

____

2. How has past abandonment shaped my expectations of God's presence?

____

____

____

____

____

3. What emotions surface for me in silence, fear, sadness, anger, uncertainty?

____

____

____

____

____

4. What truth do I need to remind myself of when silence feels threatening?

____

____

____

____

____

____

5. What would it look like to trust God's presence without demanding proof?

____

____

____

____

____

____

____

____

____

⚕ CLOSING CLINICAL NOTE

This chapter does not aim to make God louder.
It aims to make your heart safer.
God did not ghost you.
People left, and silence took on a meaning it was never meant to carry.
Healing begins when silence is no longer feared, and presence is no longer measured by noise

DR. PATRICIA S. TANNER

PERSONAL NOTES

Chapter 3

"Stop Calling It Discernment, You're Just Guarded"

SYMPTOM: When Survival Starts Pretending To Be Spiritual Wisdom

There is a point in healing where protection quietly masquerades as discernment. It happens slowly, almost responsibly. You tell yourself you are wiser now, more careful, more spiritually mature. You say you are no longer naïve, no longer easily attached, no longer vulnerable to disappointment. And while some of that may be true, there is often something else underneath it, something signalized not by clarity, but by fear.

This symptom shows up when your boundaries stop being intentional and start being automatic. When you no longer ask, *"Is this safe?"* but instead assume, *"This will end anyway."* It shows up when you read people quickly, distance yourself faster, and preemptively detach before anyone gets close enough to matter. You call it discernment because that sounds holy. But what you are really practicing is self-preservation shaped by loss.

Abandonment trains you to anticipate exits. It teaches you to scan for signs of withdrawal, inconsistency, or emotional risk. Over time, your nervous system learns to interpret closeness as danger and independence as peace. So, when people approach you now, even with sincerity, something inside you stays braced. You remain polite, measured, and distant, not because you lack love, but because you learned that attachment often comes with an expiration date.

This symptom is reinforced by spiritual language. You tell yourself that God has refined your standards, that you are simply "guarding your heart," that discernment means keeping people at a distance until they prove themselves. And while discernment does involve wisdom, it does not involve emotional shutdown. Wisdom discerns truth; fear avoids risk altogether.

What makes this symptom particularly difficult to confront is that it feels justified. After all, you were hurt. People left. Trust costs you something real. Of course you are cautious now. Of course you do not give access easily. The problem is not that you have boundaries, the problem is that your boundaries may no longer be serving connection. They are serving control.

You are not closed because you are arrogant. You are closed because you were wounded. And until that distinction is acknowledged, you will continue mistaking guardedness for growth, distance for maturity, and isolation for peace.

TEACHING: Discernment Protects Truth; Fear Protects Pain

Discernment and guardedness may look similar on the surface, but they are motivated by entirely different forces. Discernment is guided by clarity. Guardedness is guided by fear. Discernment invites wisdom into relationship. Guardedness keeps relationship at arm's length.

True discernment does not require emotional withdrawal. It allows closeness while remaining grounded. It evaluates character over time without assuming betrayal as the default outcome. Guardedness, on the other hand, assumes loss before trust has a chance to grow. It keeps emotional doors locked, not because someone is unsafe, but because the cost of being wrong feels too high.

Jesus modeled discernment without detachment. He knew the hearts of people around Him, yet He still allowed Himself to be present, vulnerable, and invested. He did not confuse wisdom with isolation. Even knowing He would be betrayed, He still sat at the table. That is not recklessness, that is rootedness.

Abandonment disrupts this balance. It teaches you that closeness is dangerous and that self-sufficiency is safer than interdependence. Over time, you begin to believe that needing people is weakness and that distance equals control. But discernment is not the absence of need, it is the presence of awareness.

Healing requires you to tell the truth about why you are guarded. Not to dismantle your boundaries, but to examine whether they are built on wisdom or fear. Because fear-based boundaries may protect you from pain, but they also block intimacy, connection, and growth.

You do not need to become reckless to heal.
You do not need to trust everyone.
You do not need to abandon discernment.
You do need to stop letting fear make decisions in the name of spirituality.

God does not call you to isolation disguised as wisdom. He calls you to love without losing yourself, to trust without disappearing, and to discern without assuming abandonment is inevitable.

CLINICAL NOTE (Faith Clinic Assessment)

The patient exhibits trauma-informed guardedness misidentified as spiritual discernment. Boundaries present; emotional access restricted.
Treatment will focus on restoring relational safety without dismantling wisdom.

FAITH PRESCRIPTION

Rebuilding Discernment Without Emotional Lockdown

Prescription Name: Discernment Realignment Therapy
Dosage: Applied relationally, moment by moment
Duration: Ongoing, do not discontinue when vulnerability feels uncomfortable
Refills: Unlimited

Instructions for Use:
This prescription does not ask you to tear down your boundaries. It asks you to examine what they are protecting. Boundaries rooted in wisdom allow connection to grow at a healthy pace. Boundaries rooted in fear prevent connection altogether. Each time you feel the urge to emotionally withdraw, pause and ask yourself: ***"Am I responding to the present moment, or reacting to a past wound?"***

Not every hesitation is discernment. Not every instinct is wisdom. Sometimes your body remembers abandonment before your mind recognizes safety. This prescription retrains discernment to include compassion—for yourself and for others.

You are instructed to allow gradual connection without forcing closeness or enforcing distance prematurely. Healing happens in measured trust, not total isolation.

Important Warning:
Avoid labeling emotional shutdown as spiritual maturity. Growth expands capacity; fear contracts it.

🕊 HOLY SPIRIT CONSULT

Learning to Discern Without Bracing

The Holy Spirit is not asking you to be naïve. He is asking you to be present. He knows why you learned to guard yourself. He is not criticizing your survival. He is gently inviting you to let wisdom lead instead of fear. Discernment guided by the Spirit does not close hearts, it steadies them.

You are not being called to reopen every door. You are being called to stop locking doors out of reflex. The Spirit is restoring your ability to sense truth without anticipating loss. He is teaching you that safety can be rebuilt without sacrificing self-respect.

🙏 GUIDED PRAYER

"God, I admit that I have been guarded, not because I lack wisdom, but because I was hurt. I have called fear discernment and distance maturity because it felt safer than risking connection again. I ask You now to help me tell the difference between wisdom and protection rooted in pain.

Teach me how to discern without withdrawing.
Teach me how to trust without disappearing.
Teach me how to set boundaries without building walls.
I release the need to control outcomes.
I release the belief that closeness always ends in loss.
I choose to let wisdom, not fear, lead my relationships.
Amen."

📝 JOURNAL REFLECTION PAGE

Take your time with these questions. There is no rush.

1.   What situations cause me to emotionally withdraw the fastest?

____

____

____

____

____

2.   How do I usually justify my guardedness?

____

____

____

____

____

3.   What am I afraid would happen if I stayed open a little longer?

____

____

____

____

____

4.   Where might fear be masquerading as discernment in my life?

____

____

____

____

____

5. What would it look like to practice wisdom without emotional
    shutdown?

____

____

____

____

____

____

____

____

____

____

____

____

____

____

⚕ CLOSING CLINICAL NOTE

This chapter does not accuse you of being closed.
It honors that you were hurt and invites you to heal without hiding.
Discernment is meant to guide connection, not eliminate it.
You are not wrong for being careful.
You are healing by learning when caution becomes isolation.

Chapter 4

"Loyalty That Cost You Yourself"

SYMPTOM: When Staying Became A Substitute For Being Chosen

There is a kind of loyalty that looks noble from the outside but slowly erodes you from the inside. It is loyalty that keeps showing up even when the relationship has stopped being mutual. The loyalty  that absorbs inconsistency, excuses disrespect and tolerates emotional absence in the name of commitment. You did not stay because it was healthy. You stayed because leaving felt like failure, and being left once already hurt enough.

This symptom is common in people who have experienced abandonment.

When you have been left before, you learn to equate staying with safety. You believe that if you can just endure long enough, prove your worth consistently enough, or love deeply enough, the relationship will stabilize. Loyalty becomes your insurance policy against being abandoned again.

So, you stay longer than your spirit can sustain. You explain away behavior that hurts you. You accept crumbs because you remember seasons when there was nothing at all. You tell yourself that relationships require sacrifice, without noticing that you are always the one being sacrificed.

This symptom is reinforced by spiritual language. Loyalty is praised. Endurance is celebrated. Faithfulness is preached. But no one ever teaches you how to discern when loyalty turns into self-betrayal. No one explains that staying is not always obedience, and leaving is not always rebellion. So, you carry the weight of relationships God never asked you to maintain alone.

Over time, this kind of loyalty costs you your voice. You stop expressing disappointment because it feels inconvenient. You stop naming needs because you fear rocking the boat. You stop being honest because honesty might push someone away. And because you are strong, capable, and faithful, no one notices the quiet erosion happening beneath the surface.

You are not loyal because you lack wisdom. You are loyal because you were afraid of being left again. And until that fear is acknowledged, loyalty will continue to drain you instead of ground you.

TEACHING: Loyalty Is Not The Same As Self-Sacrifice Without Consent

Biblical loyalty was never meant to require self-erasure. It was designed to operate within mutual commitment, shared responsibility, and truth. Loyalty becomes destructive when it is one-sided, fear-driven, and disconnected from reality. Staying in a relationship does not make it holy if it requires you to disappear.

Jesus modeled commitment without self-abandonment. He loved deeply, served faithfully, and remained present, but He did not chase people who chose to leave. He did not beg for loyalty, and He did not sacrifice His mission to maintain proximity with those unwilling to walk in truth. He let people choose, and He honored their choices without internalizing them as rejection.

Abandonment distorts loyalty by turning it into a defense mechanism. You stay not because the relationship is healthy, but because leaving feels unsafe. You confuse endurance with faithfulness and endurance becomes a way to avoid grief. If you never leave, you never have to face the pain of another goodbye.

But loyalty that costs you your peace, your voice, and your sense of self is not love, it is fear wearing devotion as a disguise. God does not ask you to remain in relationships that require you to shrink. He does not ask you to tolerate emotional absence in exchange for proximity. He does not equate suffering with faithfulness. There is a difference between covenant and captivity, between commitment and self-neglect.

Healing requires you to redefine loyalty, not as staying at all costs, but as honoring truth, mutuality, and alignment. Loyalty is not proven by how much you endure. It is proven by how well you remain whole.

You are not disloyal for walking away from what drains you. You are not unfaithful for choosing health. You are not failing God by refusing to abandon yourself.

CLINICAL NOTE (Faith Clinic Assessment)

The patient exhibits fear-based loyalty rooted in abandonment trauma. Relational endurance exceeds mutual investment. Treatment will focus on restoring self-honor and redefining loyalty through truth and alignment.

FAITH PRESCRIPTION

Reclaiming Loyalty Without Self-Erasure

Prescription Name: Relational Equity Therapy
Dosage: Applied consistently in all relationships
Duration: Ongoing, especially during seasons of transition
Refills: Unlimited

Instructions for Use:

This prescription invites you to evaluate loyalty through balance rather than endurance. Loyalty is not measured by how long you stay, but by whether the relationship honors truth, responsibility, and mutual care.

Each time you feel compelled to stay despite emotional cost, ask yourself: *"Am I choosing this relationship, or am I afraid of losing it?"*

You are instructed to stop equating longevity with health. Time invested does not oblige you to remain in something that no longer serves growth. Love does not require self-neglect as proof. Healing loyalty means learning how to leave without shame when alignment is gone and staying without fear when connection is mutual.

Important Warning:
Avoid using loyalty to avoid grief. Unprocessed loss will always resurface elsewhere.

🕊 HOLY SPIRIT CONSULT

Learning When Staying Is No Longer Obedience
- ✓ The Holy Spirit is not accusing you of staying too long. He understands why you did.
- ✓ He sees the fear that drove your endurance and the hope that kept you trying. He is not asking you to regret your loyalty, He is asking you to stop paying for it with your identity.
- ✓ The Spirit is restoring discernment to loyalty. He is teaching you that obedience sometimes looks like releasing what you were never meant to carry alone.
- ✓ You are not selfish.
- ✓ You are being honest.

🙏 GUIDED PRAYER

"God, I admit that I stayed in places that slowly emptied me because

leaving felt more painful than enduring.
I have confused loyalty with self-sacrifice and faithfulness with silence. I ask You now to heal the part of me that believed staying was the only way to remain safe.
Teach me how to honor relationships without dishonoring myself.
Teach me how to release what no longer aligns without guilt.
Teach me how to trust that obedience does not require self-erasure.
I give You permission to redefine loyalty in my life.
I choose wholeness over fear-driven endurance.
Amen."

📝 JOURNAL REFLECTION PAGE

Answer these questions honestly and without rushing.
1. Where in my life have I stayed longer than alignment allowed?

____

____

____

____

____

2. What did staying protect me from feeling or facing?

____

____

____

____

____

3. How has loyalty cost me my voice, peace, or authenticity?

____

____

____

____

____

4. What fears surface when I imagine choosing myself?

____

____

____

____

____

5. What would healthy, mutual loyalty look like for me now?

____

____

____

____

____

____

⚕ CLOSING CLINICAL NOTE

This chapter does not condemn your loyalty.
It honors your heart and restores your boundaries.
You were not wrong for staying.
You are healing by learning when staying costs too much.
Loyalty was never meant to require losing yourself.

PERSONAL NOTES

____

____

____

____

____

____

____

____

____

____

Chapter 5

"Being 'Low Maintenance' Is Not a Calling"

SYMPTOM: When Minimizing Yourself Feels Safer Than Being Honest

Somewhere along the way, you learned that needing less made you easier to keep. You stopped asking questions. You stopped expressing disappointment. You stopped sharing what you wanted or needed. Not because those needs disappeared, but because you learned that expressing them often led to distance, discomfort, or abandonment. So, you adapted.

You became "low maintenance."

At first, it felt empowering. You told yourself you were independent, flexible, easygoing, spiritually mature. You didn't require much reassurance. You didn't ask for constant communication. You didn't need emotional check-ins or clarity. You told yourself that people were busy, that expectations were unrealistic, that asking for more might push them away.

What you didn't realize at the time was that you were slowly training yourself to disappear. This symptom shows up when you pride yourself on not needing much from anyone. When you apologize for normal emotions. When you downplay disappointment before anyone else has a chance to dismiss it. You tell yourself you're being understanding, but what you are really doing is preemptively abandoning your own needs so no one else must.

Abandonment teaches you that need is dangerous. It convinces you that the more self-sufficient you appear, the safer you will be. So you learn how to carry emotional weight quietly. You learn how to show up for others without asking them to show up for you. You learn how to survive without being supported, and then you call it strength.

This symptom is especially reinforced in faith spaces. Neediness is often confused with immaturity. Independence is praised. Sacrifice is glorified. So you spiritualize self-neglect and call it humility. You convince yourself that wanting consistency, clarity, or care is asking too much.

But the truth is simpler and harder to admit: you learned to be low maintenance because high need once cost you people. You are not easygoing by nature. You are exhausted from being disappointed. And until that is named, you will continue shrinking yourself in relationships, not because you lack value, but because you are afraid of being left again.

TEACHING: Need Does Not Make You A Burden

God never designed human beings to be emotionally self-sustaining. Need is not a flaw; it is a feature. It is part of how connection works. Healthy relationships require mutual expression, mutual care, and mutual responsibility. When one person carries all the weight quietly, the relationship becomes unbalanced, even if it looks peaceful on the surface. 

Jesus never shamed people for having needs. He did not tell the hungry to stop asking for bread or the grieving to stop weeping. He did not reward emotional silence or praise people for disappearing. He met need with presence, not criticism.

Abandonment distorts this truth. It teaches you that expressing need increases risk. It tells you that if you can just want less, expect less, and ask for less, you will finally be safe. But safety built on self-denial is fragile. It requires constant suppression, constant monitoring, and constant restraint.

Being low maintenance does not make you spiritually mature. It makes you unseen. God does not ask you to eliminate your needs to be loved. He invites you to bring them honestly, without apology. Relationships that cannot hold your needs without resentment or withdrawal are not being tested by your honesty; they are being revealed by it.

Healing means learning how to express need without equating it with danger. It means allowing yourself to take up space again, emotionally and relationally. It means trusting that being honest about what you need does not make you difficult, it makes you real.

You are not asking for too much.
You are asking the wrong people to carry it.

And until you stop shrinking yourself to maintain proximity, you will continue mistaking emotional deprivation for peace.

CLINICAL NOTE: (Faith Clinic Assessment)

- ✓ Patient exhibits chronic need suppression rooted in abandonment trauma.
- ✓ Emotional self-minimization present.
- ✓ Treatment will focus on restoring permission to need without fear of rejection.

⚕ FAITH PRESCRIPTION

Relearning How To Need Without Apologizing

Prescription Name: Emotional Permission Therapy
Dosage: Practiced relationally, especially in safe connections

Duration: Ongoing; do not discontinue when discomfort arises
Refills: Unlimited

Instructions for Use:
This prescription invites you to stop apologizing for being human. You are instructed to notice how often you minimize your needs before anyone else has a chance to respond. Pay attention to how quickly you say, "It's fine," when it isn't.

Each time you feel the urge to downplay a need, ask yourself: *"What am I afraid would happen if I were honest?"*

Needing does not make you weak. Suppressing need does not make you strong. Healing requires courage—not the courage to endure quietly, but the courage to speak honestly and remain present regardless of the outcome.

Important Warning:
Avoid equating emotional independence with health. Isolation disguised as strength delays healing.

🕊 HOLY SPIRIT CONSULT

Restoring Permission to Be Human
The Holy Spirit is not disappointed by your needs. He is grieved by how long you've denied them.

He understands why you learned to minimize yourself. He knows how abandonment trained you to survive quietly. He is not asking you to become demanding, He is inviting you to become honest.
You do not have to earn care by being easy.
You do not have to disappear to be kept.
You do not have to shrink to belong.
The Spirit is restoring your permission to take up space again.

🙏 GUIDED PRAYER

"God, I confess that I learned to need less so I wouldn't lose people. I minimized my feelings, silenced my desires, and called it maturity because it felt safer than risking rejection. I ask You now to heal the part of me that believes my needs are a burden.
Teach me how to express what I need without fear.
Teach me how to trust that honesty will not always lead to loss.
Teach me how to take up space without guilt.
I release the lie that being low maintenance makes me lovable.
I choose truth over self-erasure.
I choose honesty over fear.
Amen."

📝 JOURNAL REFLECTION PAGE

Take your time with these questions.
1. What needs do I minimize most often?

____

____

____

____

____

2. What do I fear would happen if I expressed them honestly?

____

____

____

____

____

____

3. Who taught me that needing less was safer?

____

____

____

____

____

4. How has being "low maintenance" cost me emotionally?

____

____

____

____

____

5. What would it look like to take up space without apology?

____

____

____

____

____

____

℞ CLOSING CLINICAL NOTE

This chapter does not shame your adaptability.
It honors your survival and calls you into fullness.
You were not meant to be easy to keep.
You were meant to be known.
And healing begins when you stop shrinking yourself to stay connected.

PERSONAL NOTES

Part 2

THE SYMPTOMS

PERSONAL NOTES

Chapter 6

"Hyper-Independent, But Still Hurting"

SYMPTOM: When Self-Reliance Becomes A Trauma Response

You didn't wake up one day and decide to stop needing people. You learned it. You earned it. You adapted into it. Hyper-independence did not come from pride; it came from disappointment. It formed after enough unmet expectations, broken promises, and quiet exits convinced you that relying on anyone else was a gamble you could no longer afford.

So, you became capable. Resourceful. Self-sufficient. You figured things out alone because no one else was consistent enough to count on. You stopped asking for help because asking often led to silence, delay, or disappointment. Somewhere along the way, doing everything yourself stopped feeling impressive and started feeling necessary.

This symptom shows up when people praise your strength, but no one sees your exhaustion. It shows up when you are the one others lean on, but you do not know who to lean on yourself. It shows up when receiving help makes you uncomfortable, suspicious, or emotionally tense—because needing others once hurts too much.

Abandonment teaches you a dangerous equation: ***dependence equals risk***.

So, you eliminate the risk by eliminating dependence. You learn to handle life on your own, not because you want to, but because it feels safer than hoping someone else will show up.

The problem is that hyper-independence does not heal abandonment. It manages it. It keeps you functioning, but it also keeps you isolated. You may appear strong on the outside, but internally you are tired of carrying everything alone. You long for connection, yet the idea of relying on someone feels foreign, uncomfortable, or even threatening.

This symptom is often reinforced by faith language. Strength is praised. Endurance is celebrated. Self-sacrifice is honored. So your isolation looks spiritual instead of wounded. You convince yourself that God is all you need, while quietly resenting the fact that no one else stayed.

You are not independent because you are superior. You are independent because you were left to fend for yourself. And until that truth is acknowledged, independence will continue protecting you from pain while also preventing you from being supported.

TEACHING: Self-Reliance Is Not The Same As Strength

Strength in Scripture was never meant to be solitary. God consistently designed healing, growth, and endurance to happen in community. Even Jesus, fully capable and fully divine, did not walk alone. He invited others into His life, shared burdens, and allowed Himself to be supported, despite knowing some would fail Him.

Hyper-independence confuses capability with health. Yes, you can do things alone. Yes, you have proven that. But the ability to survive without support does not mean you were meant to. Self-reliance born from abandonment is not strength, it is armor.

God does not ask you to carry everything by yourself as proof of faith. He invites you to trust Him *and* receive support. Healing does not require you to abandon independence altogether, but it does require you to loosen its grip. True strength is not refusing help; it is discerning when to receive it.

Abandonment trained you to believe that depending on others would only lead to disappointment. But that belief keeps you in control at the cost of connection. Control feels safe, but it is not the same as peace. Peace allows room for interdependence without fear of collapse.

You are not weak in needing people.
You are not failing to want support.
You are not ungodly for desiring connection.

God does not replace people; He restores your capacity to trust again, slowly, wisely, and without shame. Healing means learning how to let support in without surrendering your discernment. It means allowing yourself to be helped without feeling indebted, exposed, or foolish. It means believing that receiving care does not make you vulnerable to abandonment, it makes you human.

CLINICAL NOTE (Faith Clinic Assessment)

Patient exhibits hyper-independence rooted in abandonment trauma. Functional resilience present; relational support limited. Treatment will focus on restoring safe dependence without compromising autonomy.

FAITH PRESCRIPTION

Learning How to Receive Without Losing Yourself

Prescription Name: Interdependence Rehabilitation
Dosage: Gradual, one safe interaction at a time
Duration: Ongoing; do not discontinue when discomfort arises
Refills: Unlimited

Instructions for Use:
This prescription does not require you to suddenly trust everyone. It invites you to identify *safe* people and allow measured support.

Healing independence means learning how to receive without feeling weak, exposed, or obligated.

Each time you feel the urge to do everything alone, pause and ask: *"Am I choosing independence, or am I avoiding disappointment?"*

Practice receiving small forms of help without explaining yourself or minimizing your need. Allow support without rushing to reciprocate or prove your worth.

Important Warning:
Avoid equating control with safety. Control may prevent pain, but it also prevents connection.

🕊 HOLY SPIRIT CONSULT

Releasing Control Without Fear
The Holy Spirit understands why you became independent. He is not asking you to regret your survival. He is inviting you to release the belief that you must carry everything alone to remain safe.

He is teaching you that trust can be rebuilt without abandoning wisdom. That receiving does not mean losing control. That vulnerability does not guarantee loss.

You do not have to do everything alone anymore.
You do not have to prove your strength by suffering silently.
You are allowed to be supported.

🙏 GUIDED PRAYER

"God, I admit that I learned to rely only on myself because relying on others once hurt too much. I have carried burdens alone because it felt safer than hoping someone would stay. I ask You now to heal the part of me that believes independence is my only protection.

Teach me how to receive without fear.
Teach me how to trust without surrendering wisdom.
Teach me how to rest without feeling irresponsible.
I release the need to control everything.
I open myself to safe support.
I choose connection without shame.
Amen."

📝 JOURNAL REFLECTION PAGE

Answer honestly and without rushing.

1. What situations trigger my need to handle everything alone?

____

____

____

____

____

2. Who taught me that needing help was unsafe?

____

____

____

____

____

3. How has hyper-independence protected me and how has it cost me?

____

____

____

____

____

____

4.   What support do I secretly wish I had right now?

____

____

____

____

____

____

5.   What would it look like to receive help without guilt or fear?

____

____

____

____

____

____

____

____

⚕ CLOSING CLINICAL NOTE

This chapter does not diminish your strength.
It reframes it.
You survived because you had to.
Now you are healing so you do not have to do it alone anymore.
Strength was never meant to isolate you.
It was meant to carry you into connection.

PERSONAL NOTES

____

____

____

____

____

____

____

____

____

____

____

Chapter 7

"Leaving First So It Hurts Less"

SYMPTOM: When Pre-Emptive Distance Feels Like Control

At some point, abandonment stopped feeling like a shock and started feeling like a pattern. You noticed the warning signs early, the shift in tone, the delay in response, the subtle emotional withdrawal. And instead of waiting for the moment, it finally happened, you learned how to exit quietly first. Not dramatically. Not angrily. Just emotionally.

This symptom shows up when you pull back before anyone can pull away from you. When you detach internally while still showing up externally. When you stop investing, stop hoping, and stop expecting, not because the relationship is over, but because you are preparing for the pain you believe is coming.

Leaving first gives you the illusion of control. It feels proactive. It feels protective. It feels safer than being blindsided again. You tell yourself that you are simply being realistic, that you are reading the room accurately, that you are sparing yourself unnecessary hurt. But what you are really doing is grieving relationships before they are finished.

 Abandonment trains you to expect endings. So instead of allowing closeness to develop naturally, you monitor it. You stay alert. You anticipate loss. You emotionally pack your bags long before anything falls apart. And when distance finally happens, you tell yourself you were right all along.

This symptom is reinforced by pride masquerading as wisdom. You convince yourself that leaving first makes you strong, that it proves you are not desperate, that it protects your dignity. But beneath that posture is fear, not fear of rejection, but fear of hope. Because hope makes loss hurt more.

You are not cold.
You are cautious.
You are not indifferent.
You are tired of being surprised by pain.
And until this pattern is named, you will continue leaving relationships emotionally long before they ever leave you physically.

TEACHING: Control Is Not The Same As Safety

Leaving first may feel like protection, but it is a form of self-abandonment. It disconnects you from the present moment in order to avoid a future pain that has not yet occurred. It trades intimacy for anticipation and replaces connection with caution.

Jesus did not leave relationships early to avoid betrayal. He remained present even when the risk was real. He did not detach to protect Himself from pain; He trusted God to hold Him through it. That does not mean He ignored red flags or tolerated abuse, it means He did not let fear dictate when love ended.

Abandonment convinces you that staying open is irresponsible. It teaches you that the sooner you detach, the less it will hurt. But pain avoided is not pain healed. It simply resurfaces later, often in the form of loneliness, regret, or emotional numbness.

God does not call you to abandon relationships prematurely to avoid disappointment. He calls you to remain present, honest, and grounded, without attaching your worth to outcomes. Staying present does not guarantee people will stay, but leaving first guarantees that connection never has a chance.

You are allowed to leave relationships that are harmful, unsafe, or misaligned. That is not what this chapter addresses. This chapter addresses leaving out of fear, leaving before clarity, leaving before truth, leaving before love has had a chance to prove itself. You do not heal abandonment by beating people to the exit. You heal it by staying rooted in yourself regardless of who stays or goes.

CLINICAL NOTE (Faith Clinic Assessment)

- ✓ The patient exhibits pre-emptive emotional detachment rooted in abandonment trauma.
- ✓ Anticipatory grief present.
- ✓ Treatment will focus on restoring presence without attachment to outcome.

⊘ FAITH PRESCRIPTION

Learning How to Stay Without Bracing for Loss

Prescription Name: Present-Moment Attachment Therapy
Dosage: Applied relationally, one interaction at a time
Duration: Ongoing—do not discontinue when anxiety rises
Refills: Unlimited

Instructions for Use:
This prescription does not require you to stay in unhealthy relationships. It requires you to stop leaving *healthy* ones out of fear. You are instructed to notice when you emotionally disengage before anything has gone wrong.

Each time you feel the urge to pull away, ask yourself: *"Am I responding to what is happening, or reacting to what once happened?"*

Practice remaining present without forecasting loss. Allow relationships to reveal themselves in real time rather than through anticipation.

Important Warning:

Avoid confusing intuition with anxiety. Anxiety predicts harm; wisdom discerns reality.

☙ HOLY SPIRIT CONSULT

Choosing Presence Over Protection

The Holy Spirit is not pressuring you to stay where you are unsafe. He is inviting you to stop leaving places where nothing has broken yet.
He understands why you learned to exit early. He sees the fear beneath your detachment. And He is gently teaching you that you do not need to outrun pain to be protected.
God is not asking you to guarantee outcomes.
He is asking you to remain present and truthful.
You do not have to abandon yourself to stay connected.
You do not have to leave early to remain whole.

🙏 GUIDED PRAYER

'God, I admit that I have learned to leave first so it would hurt less. I have detached emotionally before relationships ended because hope felt too risky. I ask You now to heal the part of me that believes presence is dangerous.

Teach me how to stay present without bracing for loss. Teach me how to trust the moment without predicting the ending. Teach me how to love without fear controlling the timeline.

I release the need to control outcomes.
I choose presence over protection.
I trust You to hold me no matter what happens.
Amen."

📝 JOURNAL REFLECTION PAGE

Take your time with these questions.
1. When do I feel the urge to emotionally leave first?

2. What am I afraid will happen if I stay present?

3. How has leaving early protected me, and how has it cost me?

4. What relationships have I grieved before they ended?

____

____

____

____

____

____

5. What would it look like to stay grounded regardless of outcome?

____

____

____

____

____

____

____

⚕ CLOSING CLINICAL NOTE

This chapter does not accuse you of running.
It understands why you learned to.
Leaving first kept you from being blindsided.
Staying present will teach you how to live again.
You are not reckless for hoping.
You are healing by learning how to remain.

PERSONAL NOTES

Chapter 8

"Numb Isn't Peace, It's Exhaustion"

SYMPTOM: When Feeling Nothing Feels Safer Than Feeling Anything

At first, the numbness feels like relief. After so much disappointment, so many goodbyes, and so many moments where hope hurt more than it helped, not feeling anything at all can feel like progress. You tell yourself you are calmer now, less reactive, less emotional. You convince yourself that this must be peace, because the ache has dulled and the tears have slowed.

But numbness is not peace. It is the body's way of saying it cannot carry any more.

This symptom shows up when joy feels muted and grief feels distant, when you no longer feel deeply disappointed because you no longer feel deeply invested. It shows up when worship feels flat, relationships feel neutral, and life feels manageable, but hollow. You are functioning, but you are not fully alive.

Abandonment overloads the nervous system. Each loss, each departure, each emotional rupture adds weight. Eventually, your system does what it must to survive, it shuts down sensation to conserve energy. Numbness is not a decision you made; it is a response your body learned.

You stopped expecting too much.
You stopped hoping too hard.
You stopped feeling deeply because deep feeling came with deep loss.
And in faith spaces, numbness often gets mislabeled as maturity.
You are praised for being steady, unbothered, composed. No one notices that your steadiness came at the cost of aliveness. No one asks whether your calm is rooted in peace or depletion.
You are not healed because it doesn't hurt anymore.
You are tired of hurting.

And until that exhaustion is acknowledged, numbness will continue masquerading as peace.

TEACHING: Peace Is Alive; Numbness Is Protective

Biblical peace is not the absence of feeling; it is the presence of trust. It is steady without being empty, grounded without being detached. Peace allows joy and grief to coexist. Numbness does not allow either.

Jesus did not model emotional shutdown. He wept. He rejoiced. He grieved openly. He felt deeply without being ruled by His emotions. Emotional range was not a liability in Him; it was evidence of wholeness.

Abandonment teaches you that feeling deeply is dangerous. It convinces you that if you just stop feeling so much, you will finally be safe. But safety built on numbness is fragile. It disconnects you from pain, yes, but it also disconnects you from pleasure, intimacy, and meaning.

God does not call you to numbness. He calls you to peace. And peace does not require shutting down your heart. It requires restoring trust, slowly, gently, and without forcing emotional intensity before you are ready.

Healing from numbness is not about forcing yourself to feel again. It is about restoring capacity. It is about giving your nervous system permission to thaw at its own pace. It is about recognizing that emotional flatness is not failure, it is fatigue.

You are not broken for feeling numb.

You are depleted.

And depletion requires rest, safety, and patience, not pressure.

CLINICAL NOTE (Faith Clinic Assessment)

Patient exhibits emotional shutdown consistent with prolonged abandonment stress.
Affect flattened; capacity reduced.
Treatment will focus on nervous system regulation and gradual emotional re-engagement.

💊 FAITH PRESCRIPTION

Restoring Feeling Without Overwhelming the System

Prescription Name: Emotional Reawakening Therapy
Dosage: Gentle, incremental
Duration: Ongoing; do not rush
Refills: Unlimited

Instructions for Use:
This prescription does not ask you to feel everything at once. It asks you to notice small sensations without judgment. Healing numbness is not about intensity, it is about safety.

Each day, you are instructed to identify one moment of sensation: warmth, relief, curiosity, comfort, or even sadness. Feeling *something* is progress. Do not force joy. Do not manufacture emotion. Allow your system to lead.
Each time you feel tempted to dismiss numbness as peace, ask yourself: *"Am I calm because I trust, or because I am tired?"* Rest is not avoidance. Stillness is not stagnation. Healing begins when you stop demanding emotional performance from yourself.

Important Warning:
Avoid spiritualizing numbness. Suppression delays restoration.

🕊 HOLY SPIRIT CONSULT

Gentle Restoration, Not Forced Feeling

The Holy Spirit is not disappointed by your numbness.
He recognizes it as fatigue.
He is not pushing you to feel more.
He is inviting you to feel safe.
The Spirit restores gently. He does not rip hearts open; He rebuilds capacity. He understands that your heart shut down because it had to, not because it wanted to.
You are not distant from God because you feel numb.
You are recovering.

🙏 GUIDED PRAYER

"God, I admit that I don't feel much right now.
Not because I don't care,
but because I'm tired.
I've felt deeply for a long time, and the losses added up. I ask You to meet me here—not with pressure to feel, but with permission to rest.
Restore my capacity gently.
Teach my heart that it is safe to feel again.
Help me trust that peace does not require numbness.
I receive Your presence without striving.
I allow healing to happen at its own pace.
I choose rest over performance.
Amen."

📝 JOURNAL REFLECTION PAGE

Answer these questions slowly and without expectation.
1. When did I first notice feeling numb?

____

____

____

____

____

____

2. What losses preceded this shutdown?

____

____

____

____

____

3. How has numbness protected me?

____

____

____

____

____

4. What emotions feel hardest to access right now?

____

____

____

____

____

____

____

5. What would gentle restoration look like for me?

____

____

____

____

____

____

____

____

____

____

____

⚕ CLOSING CLINICAL NOTE

This chapter does not accuse you of being cold.
It recognizes that you are exhausted.
Numbness kept you functioning.
Healing will help you feel again, without drowning.
Peace is not emptiness.
It is trust returning.

PERSONAL NOTES

Chapter 9

"Missing People Who Didn't Choose You"

SYMPTOM: When Familiarity Feels Like Love And Absence Gets Romanticized

There is a specific kind of ache that settles in long after a relationship has ended, not because it was healthy, but because it was familiar. This ache does not always show up as longing for the person themselves. More often, it shows up as nostalgia for how things once felt, or how you hoped they might eventually feel. You miss the idea of connection more than the reality of it, but your body does not know the difference. It only knows that something once occupied space, and now that space feels empty.

This symptom is especially confusing because it does not come from denial. You are fully aware that the person did not choose you consistently. You know they were distant, inconsistent, emotionally unavailable, or unable to show up when it mattered. You are not lying to yourself about what happened. And yet, despite this clarity, you still miss them.

You miss the routine.
You miss the familiarity.
You miss the version of yourself that hoped things would change.

Abandonment creates a powerful bond between pain and memory. When someone leaves, the relationship does not simply end; it becomes unfinished. There are conversations that never happened, explanations that never came, and expectations that were never resolved. Your nervous system continues reaching for resolution, not because the relationship was good, but because it never closed properly.

So you replay moments that felt warm. You minimize the parts that hurt. You remember who they were at their best and quietly forget who they were at their worst. You do not do this intentionally. Your mind does it for you, because familiarity feels safer than uncertainty, even when that familiarity came with pain.

This symptom shows up when you find yourself missing people who repeatedly disappointed you. When you wonder why your heart aches for someone who made you feel unseen. When you question your own discernment because the longing does not match the truth you know intellectually. You ask yourself why you cannot just let go when you already understand that the relationship was misaligned.

What makes this symptom especially dangerous is that it invites self-blame. You begin to wonder what is wrong with you for missing someone who did not choose you. You assume it means you are weak, attached, or emotionally dependent. In faith spaces, you may even assume it means you have not forgiven properly or trusted God enough.

But the truth is far more human.
You are not missing the person.
You are missing the *promise* you carried.

You are grieving the version of the relationship that never had a chance to exist, the version you kept hoping would emerge if you just stayed patient enough, loving enough, or understanding enough. And because that version never arrived, your grief has nowhere to land. It lingers.

Abandonment makes familiarity feel sacred. When someone leaves, your system panics at the sudden absence. Even painful connection feels better than no connection at all, so your mind reaches backward instead of forward. It convinces you that something known, even if it hurt, is preferable to something unknown that might disappoint you again.

This is why you miss people who did not choose you. Not because they were right for you, but because losing them reopened older wounds that taught you loss equals danger. The longing is not about desire. It is about safety.

And until this is named, you will continue romanticizing absence and confusing longing with love.

TEACHING: Longing Is Not Proof Of Alignment

One of the most important distinctions healing requires is the difference between longing and alignment. Longing is emotional. Alignment is relational. Longing responds to memory, attachment, and unresolved grief. Alignment responds to truth, consistency, and mutual choice. When you confuse the two, you begin measuring compatibility by how much you miss someone instead of how well they showed up.

Scripture never teaches that longing is evidence of God's will. In fact, it often warns against returning to what is familiar simply because it feels comfortable. The Israelites longed for Egypt, not because it was good, but because it was known. Familiar suffering felt safer than unfamiliar freedom. That same pattern repeats in abandonment.

Missing someone does not mean they were meant to stay. Feeling attached does not mean the relationship was aligned. Pain does not sanctify connection.

Abandonment wires the brain to associate familiarity with survival. When someone leaves, your system searches for what it lost, even if what it lost was inconsistent or emotionally unsafe. The longing you feel is not an invitation to return; it is an echo of attachment seeking closure.

This is why healing requires honesty about what you are missing. Are you missing the person, or are you missing the role they played in your life? Are you missing them, or are you missing who you were before the disappointment set in? Are you missing connection, or are you missing validation?

God does not shame longing, but He does not allow it to rewrite truth. He does not ask you to forget the good, but He does not allow you to ignore the pattern. Healing happens when you stop editing history to make loss easier to tolerate.

The people who were aligned with you did not make you feel disposable. They did not require you to overextend to earn consistency. They did not disappear when things became inconvenient. Alignment does not exhaust you. It steadies you.

Abandonment trains you to equate intensity with connection. When someone leaves, the emotional crash creates intensity, and your body confuses that intensity with significance. But intensity is not intimacy, and longing is not love.

God does not measure relationships by how deeply you ache when they end. He measures them by truth, fruit, and mutuality. Relationships that were meant to shape you will not require you to beg, chase, or reinterpret neglect as mystery.

Letting go does not require you to stop missing someone. It requires you to stop letting the missing decide your future. Healing does not erase longing overnight. It teaches you how to hold it without obeying it.

You are allowed to grieve without returning.
You are allowed to miss without reattaching.
You are allowed to honor what was without sacrificing what could be.

Abandonment recovery is not about erasing memory. It is about restoring discernment so that longing no longer masquerades as calling.

And when you finally tell the truth—that you were not chosen, but you kept hoping, you stop asking why you miss them and start asking what you are ready to release.
That is where freedom begins.

℞ TRANSITION NOTE (Faith Clinic Continuity)

This chapter does not demand emotional detachment. It demands emotional honesty. You are not weak for missing people who did not choose you. You are healing by learning not to confuse longing with destiny.

💊 FAITH PRESCRIPTION

Detaching From Longing Without Erasing Memory

Prescription Name: Emotional Reassignment Therapy
Dosage: Daily reflection, especially when nostalgia resurfaces
Duration: Ongoing; do not discontinue when missing intensifies
Refills: Unlimited

Instructions for Use:

This prescription is not designed to eliminate longing. Longing is not the enemy. Confusion is. The goal of this treatment is to help you separate emotional attachment from relational alignment so that memory no longer dictates movement.

You are instructed to stop asking why you miss people who did not choose you and begin asking what part of you learned to survive on hope instead of reciprocity. Missing someone is not evidence that you were meant to stay connected. It is evidence that your nervous system bonded to familiarity during a season when consistency felt scarce.

Each time nostalgia pulls you backward, you are instructed to gently redirect your focus toward truth. Not harsh truth, and not self-criticism, but grounded clarity. You are not required to demonize the relationship to move on. You are only required to stop romanticizing what did not nourish you.

When the thought arises, *"Maybe it could have been different,"* you will replace it with this truth: **"What mattered most was not who they could have been, but who they consistently were."**

This prescription teaches you how to let longing exist without letting it lead. Healing does not erase desire overnight. It retrains authority.

***Important Warning*:**
Do not confuse emotional pull with divine prompting. Longing remembers; wisdom discerns.

🕊 HOLY SPIRIT CONSULT

When God Gently Corrects Without Shaming the Ache

The Holy Spirit does not rebuke you for missing people who did not choose you. He understands the ache because He understands attachment. He is not asking you to pretend the connection meant nothing. He is asking you to stop letting it define what you deserve next.

The Spirit is not trying to erase your memory. He is restoring perspective. He is reminding you that longing is not instruction and nostalgia is not confirmation. He sees how you hoped, how you waited, and how you held space for change that never came.

And without condemnation, He is saying: "I did not withhold them from you to punish you. I released them because they could not walk with you where you are going."

The Holy Spirit does not rush your grief. He walks with you through it while gently closing doors you keep revisiting out of habit. He is not offended by your feelings. He is protecting your future from being built on unresolved loss.

🙏 GUIDED PRAYER

(Honest. Grounded. No emotional performance required.)
"God, I admit that I still miss people who did not choose me.
I miss the familiarity, the hope, and the version of the story I kept believing might one day exist. I ask You to help me grieve honestly without rewriting history to make the pain feel more meaningful. Help me release the version of the relationship that never came to life.

Help me stop confusing longing with destiny.
Help me trust that what You remove is not what sustains me.
I do not want to chase what You already let go of.
I do not want to obey attachment when You are offering alignment.
I choose truth over nostalgia, even when truth feels quieter.
Hold my heart as I let go—not bitter, not hardened, but healed.
Amen."

📝 JOURNAL REFLECTION PAGE

Letting the Ache Speak Without Letting It Decide

Answer these questions slowly. Do not rush resolution.
1. Who do I miss most right now, and what do I miss about them? (Be specific. Avoid generalities.)

____

____

____

____

2. What version of the relationship am I still grieving that never fully existed?

____

____

____

____

____

3. How did I minimize inconsistency to preserve hope?

____

____

____

____

4. What has longing been protecting me from facing in the present?

____

____

____

____

____

____

5. What would it look like to honor the memory without reopening the door?

____

____

____

____

6. What kind of relationship do I now recognize as aligned, not just familiar?

____

____

____

____

℞ CLOSING CLINICAL NOTE

This chapter does not shame longing.
It restores discernment.
You were not wrong for hoping.
You are healing by learning when hope becomes self-delay.
Missing someone does not mean you should return.
It means something mattered, and now it must be released with clarity.

Part 3

THE TREATMENT PLAN

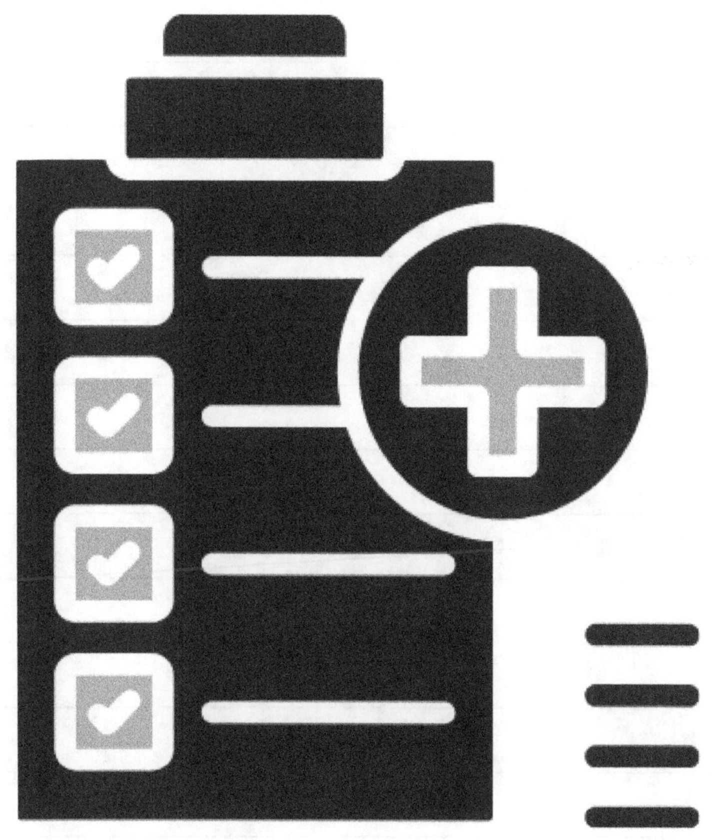

PERSONAL NOTES

Chapter 10

"God Didn't Ask You To Chase What He Already Let Go"

SYMPTOM: When Pursuit Feels Like Hope But Is Actually Fear In Motion

There is a subtle difference between faith and pursuit that abandonment blurs almost beyond recognition. Faith trusts what is unfolding. Pursuit tries to force what is fading. When abandonment has marked your history, pursuit begins to feel like responsibility. You convince yourself that if you just try harder, explain better, show up more consistently, or remain patient longer, things might finally stabilize. You tell yourself you are not chasing; you are being faithful.

But your body knows the difference, even when your theology does not.
This symptom shows up when you feel restless instead of grounded. When your energy is spent monitoring someone else's availability rather than living fully in your own life. When your peace depends on their response, their clarity, or their consistency. You are no longer present—you are pursuing.

Abandonment teaches you that relationships are fragile and fleeting, so when distance appears, your instinct is to close the gap quickly. You text again. You clarify again. You soften your needs. You make yourself more accommodating. You do not call it chasing; you call it understanding. But underneath the effort is fear, the fear that if you stop moving, you will be left behind again.

This symptom becomes especially confusing in faith spaces, because pursuit often masquerades as perseverance. You tell yourself God honors endurance. You remind yourself that love is patient. You convince yourself that waiting means working harder. But what you are really doing is attempting to control an outcome that has already begun to drift out of alignment.

You are not pursuing because you are desperate. You are pursuing because you are afraid of finality. Finality feels like abandonment. So instead of accepting what is ending, you keep the connection alive through effort, hope, and emotional labor. You become the one carrying the relationship, even when the relationship is no longer carrying you.

This symptom is exhausting. It keeps you emotionally activated and spiritually unsettled. You are never fully at rest because you are always waiting for something to shift, improve, or return. You are not living in the present; you are hovering over a possibility that no longer has roots. And because pursuit feels productive, you mistake anxiety for devotion and effort for love.

TEACHING: Faith Does Not Require You To Chase Alignment

One of the hardest truths abandonment recovery requires is this: God does not ask you to chase what He has already released. Alignment does not require pursuit. Mutuality does not require convincing. Relationships that are meant to grow do not depend on one person running toward another who is standing still or walking away. 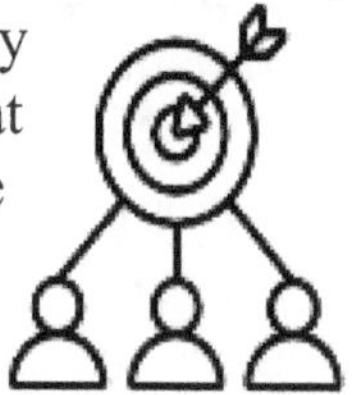

Throughout Scripture, God invites people into alignment, not pursuit. He opens doors; He does not ask you to force them. When something is sustained by God, it does not require relentless effort to remain intact. That does not mean relationships are effortless, but it does mean they are shared.

Abandonment confuses effort with faith. It teaches you that if you stop pursuing, everything will collapse. But faith is not anxious movement. Faith is trust in what is true—even when that truth is painful.

God is not honored by you chasing people who cannot meet you with clarity, consistency, or commitment. He is not impressed by emotional overextension. He does not reward self-abandonment disguised as devotion. When God releases something from your life, He does so to restore balance, not to test your endurance.

 Letting go is not quitting. It is consenting to reality.

Healing requires you to recognize when pursuit has replaced peace. When your spiritual language is covering emotional fear. When your effort is sustaining something God has already stopped feeding. That recognition is not failure, it is wisdom.

God does not ask you to prove your worth by how long you can chase. He does not measure love by emotional depletion. He measures alignment by truth, fruit, and reciprocity. If you are the only one reaching, explaining, waiting, and adjusting, you are not in alignment, you are in pursuit.

And pursuit will always drain you, because it is fueled by fear of loss rather than trust in provision. You do not heal abandonment by holding on tighter. You heal it by learning when to release without collapsing.

God is not asking you to stop caring.
He is asking you to stop chasing.
Because chasing keeps you oriented toward what is leaving, while healing reorients you toward what is being prepared.

☤ TRANSITION NOTE (Faith Clinic Continuity)

This chapter does not accuse you of trying too hard.
It understands why you did.
Pursuit felt safer than acceptance.
Chasing felt better than grieving.

Healing will teach you how to stop running after what God has already placed down, and how to stand still without fear.

FAITH PRESCRIPTION

Ending Pursuit Without Losing Hope

Prescription Name: Release-and-Realignment Therapy
Dosage: Daily practice during moments of emotional pull or urgency
Duration: Ongoing; do not discontinue when discomfort rises
Refills: Unlimited

Instructions for Use:

This prescription is not asking you to stop caring. It is asking you to stop chasing. Caring can exist without pursuit. Love can exist without self-erasure. Faith can exist without anxiety-driven motion. You are instructed to observe how often urgency appears when something is slipping away. Notice how quickly you move into explanation, clarification, accommodation, or effort. This urgency is not spiritual prompting. It is fear responding to the threat of finality.

Each time you feel the impulse to chase, pause and ask yourself: *"What am I afraid will happen if I stop reaching?"*

The answer will almost always reveal an old abandonment wound, not a present assignment.

This prescription teaches you to replace pursuit with presence. Instead of moving toward what is drifting, you will remain grounded where you are. You will allow truth to surface without interference. What stays without pursuit is aligned. What requires chasing is already misaligned.

<h1 style="text-align:center">DR. PATRICIA S. TANNER</h1>

Important Warning:
Do not confuse stillness with passivity. Stillness is an act of trust, not resignation.

🕊 HOLY SPIRIT CONSULT

When God Calls You to Stop Running

The Holy Spirit is not frustrated with your effort.
He understands why you ran toward what felt like it was slipping away.

He sees the seasons where holding on felt like survival. He remembers the losses that taught you momentum was safer than acceptance. And with compassion—not correction—He is now asking you to stop.

Not because you failed.
Not because you did not love well enough.
But because chasing is costing you peace He never intended you to lose.

The Spirit is gently saying:
"What is meant to stay will not require you to exhaust yourself.
What I have released does not need to be retrieved.
What I am aligning will meet you without pursuit."

He is not asking you to shut down your heart. He is asking you to place it back in truth instead of tension. He is restoring your dignity by teaching you that worth is not proven through pursuit.

🙏 GUIDED PRAYER

(Grounded. Honest. Unrushed.)
"God, I admit that I have chased what was already slipping away.
I called it faith, patience, and perseverance, but underneath it was
fear, fear of being left, fear of endings, fear of starting over. I ask

You now to heal the part of me that believes I must pursue to remain chosen.
Help me stop reaching for what You have already released.
Help me trust that what belongs with me will meet me without effort.
Help me remain present instead of reactive.
I release urgency.
I release the need to convince.
I release the belief that chasing proves my worth.
I choose alignment over attachment.
I choose peace over pursuit.
I trust You with what I no longer hold.
Amen."

📝 JOURNAL REFLECTION PAGE

Reclaiming Dignity Where Chasing Once Lived

Write slowly. Let truth surface without editing.

1. Who or what have I been chasing to avoid finality?

____

____

____

____

____

2. What fear rises in me when I imagine stopping pursuit completely?

____

____

____

____

____

3.   How has chasing affected my peace, focus, and sense of self?

____

____

____

____

4.   What evidence do I have that alignment does not require pursuit?

____

____

____

____

5.   What would it look like to stand still and allow truth to reveal itself?

____

____

____

____

____

6. What part of my identity do I need to reclaim now that I am no longer chasing?

____

____

____

____

____

____

____

____

____

____

____

____

____

⚕ CLOSING CLINICAL NOTE

This chapter does not shame your effort.
It restores your dignity.
You chased because you were afraid of being left again.
You are healing by learning how to stop without collapsing.
God did not ask you to chase what He already let go.
He is asking you to trust what will meet you where you stand.

PERSONAL NOTES

Chapter 11

"Closure Is Overrated; Peace Is Not" *Why You Don't Need Answers To Move Forward*

SYMPTOM: When You Keep Waiting For An Explanation That Will Never Come

One of the quietest ways abandonment keeps control over you is by convincing you that healing is impossible without closure. You tell yourself that if you could just understand why they left, why things changed, or what you missed, you would finally be able to move on. You replay conversations in your mind, search for hidden meanings, and revisit memories, hoping they will suddenly rearrange themselves into something that makes sense.

This symptom does not look dramatic. It looks thoughtful. It looks introspective. It looks like someone trying to be responsible with their emotions. But beneath the surface, it keeps you emotionally tethered to people who are no longer participating in your life.

Abandonment often ends without explanation. There is no final conversation, no honest confession, no clarity offered. People disappear, emotionally withdraw, or give vague reasons that do not match the depth of the loss. And because your brain is wired to seek meaning, it refuses to accept ambiguity. It tells you that without answers, you cannot heal. So you wait.

You wait for accountability.
You wait for an apology.
You wait for someone to finally explain what you did wrong.
And while you wait, your life remains paused around a moment that is no longer happening.

This symptom becomes especially painful because it feels reasonable. Wanting clarity is human. Wanting to understand what hurts you is not weakness. But when closure becomes a requirement instead of hope, it turns into a trap. It hands power back to people who have already left by making your peace dependent on their participation.

Abandonment teaches you that unanswered questions are dangerous. It convinces you that if you move forward without answers, you are being careless, avoidant, or dishonest with yourself. So you keep reopening wounds, not to heal them, but to examine them one more time—just in case this time the pain explains itself.

The truth is harder to accept: some people will never give you clarity because they never had it themselves. Some departures were not carefully reasoned decisions; they were reactions, limitations, or avoidances. And waiting for insight from someone who could not communicate honestly in the relationship will only prolong your confusion.

You are not stuck because you lack information. You are stuck because you were taught that peace requires permission from the person who hurt you.

TEACHING: Peace Is Not A Reward for Understanding Everything

One of the most liberating truths abandonment recovery offers is this: peace does not come from answers; it comes from acceptance. Acceptance does not mean approval. It means acknowledging what is without insisting it become something else before you move forward.

Scripture never teaches that closure is a prerequisite for healing. In fact, many biblical stories end without explanation. People leave, betray, deny, or disappear, and God does not always fill in the blanks. Instead, He invites His people to keep walking without full understanding, trusting that clarity is not the same thing as wholeness.

Abandonment tempts you to believe that answers will heal you. But answers rarely satisfy the deeper ache. Even when explanations are given, they often create more questions. Healing does not come from knowing *why* someone left; it comes from deciding what you will carry forward.

Peace is not the absence of questions. It is the absence of self-accusation.

God does not require you to understand every ending to bless your next beginning. He does not ask you to interrogate the past until it confesses. He asks you to release what no longer belongs to you, especially the responsibility to make sense of someone else's choices.

Closure implies something neat and final. Peace is often quieter and less dramatic. Peace comes when you stop needing the past to explain itself and start trusting yourself again. It comes when you realize that unanswered questions do not invalidate your experience. They simply mean you were dealing with someone who could not meet you in truth.

You do not need answers to stop blaming yourself. You do not need explanations to reclaim your dignity. You do not need closure to move forward with integrity.

Abandonment recovery is not about tying up loose ends. It is about loosening your grip on the need to control the narrative. When you release the demand for closure, you also release the hope that the past will suddenly make sense. And in that release, something unexpected happens: peace begins to form.

Not because everything is resolved, but because you stop asking broken relationships to complete you. Peace is not passive. It is a decision to stop waiting. And once you stop waiting for answers, you realize you were never stuck, you were just paused by expectation.

⚕ TRANSITION NOTE (Faith Clinic Continuity)

This chapter does not dismiss your need for understanding. It frees you from depending on it. You were not denied closure because you were unworthy. You were denied because not everyone is capable of honesty. Peace does not require permission from the past. It requires trust in yourself again.

💊 FAITH PRESCRIPTION

Choosing Peace Without Permission

Prescription Name: Acceptance Without Explanation Therapy
Dosage: Daily, especially when the urge to revisit the past resurfaces
Duration: Ongoing; do not discontinue when questions arise
Refills: Unlimited

***Instructions for Use*:**

This prescription does not deny your desire for clarity. It acknowledges it, and then gently removes it from the driver's seat. Wanting answers is human. Requiring them to move forward is what keeps you stuck.

You are instructed to stop reopening emotional files that no longer belong to you. Each time your mind circles back to the unanswered "why," you will redirect yourself to a more grounding question: ***"What do I need now to live in peace?"***

Closure is often framed as an external event, something someone else gives you through apology, explanation, or acknowledgment. This prescription reframes closure as an internal decision. You do not need consensus with the past to move forward. You only need consent from yourself.

When the thought arises, *"I can't heal without understanding,"* you will replace it with this truth: *"I can heal without answers because my worth was never dependent on them."*

Peace does not require resolution. It requires release.

Important Warning:

Avoid using analysis to delay acceptance. Overthinking is not processing when it prevents movement.

🕊 HOLY SPIRIT CONSULT

When God Invites You to Stop Waiting

The Holy Spirit is not withholding clarity from you.
He is protecting you from becoming dependent on it.
He knows that answers would not bring the relief you imagine. He understands that explanations from people who could not love you well would not suddenly heal the wound. And without judgment, He is gently inviting you to step out of waiting mode.

The Spirit is saying: "You do not need their words to validate your experience. You do not need their understanding to trust your own. You do not need their apology to move forward in peace."

God is not asking you to forget what happened. He is asking you to stop letting unanswered questions sit in the place where peace belongs. He is restoring your confidence, not by filling in the blanks, but by teaching you how to walk without them.

🙏 GUIDED PRAYER

(Grounded. Honest. Complete.)
"God, I admit that I have been waiting for answers I may never receive. I wanted explanations to justify my pain, clarity to settle my confusion, and acknowledgment to validate what I experienced. I now see that waiting for those things has kept me tethered to a past that no longer holds my future.

Help me release the need for closure.
Help me trust myself without confirmation.
Help me move forward without rehearsing what I never received.
I place unanswered questions back into Your hands.
I stop asking broken relationships to explain my worth.
I choose peace, even if nothing is resolved.
I trust that You can heal what was never explained.
I trust that peace does not require permission.
I trust myself again.
Amen."

📝 JOURNAL REFLECTION PAGE

Letting Go of the Need to Know

Answer slowly. Do not rush to resolution.

1. What answers have I been waiting for, and who am I waiting to receive them from?

____

____

____

____

____

____

2. How has waiting for closure delayed my healing or decision-making?

____

____

____

____

____

3. What emotions surface when I imagine moving forward without answers?

____

____

____

____

____

4. What would peace look like if I stopped waiting for explanation?

____

____

____

____

____

5.   What truth do I already know that I have been avoiding
      because it feels final?

____

____

____

____

____

6.   What permission do I need to give myself today?

____

____

____

____

____

____

____

℞ CLOSING CLINICAL NOTE

This chapter does not minimize your desire for clarity.
It releases you from being ruled by it.
You were not denied closure because you were unworthy.
You were denied it because not everyone is capable of truth.
Peace does not arrive with explanations.
It arrives when you stop waiting.
You are free to move forward, whole, grounded, and no longer asking
the past to explain itself.

PERSONAL NOTES

Chapter 12

"Trusting Again Without Abandoning Yourself"

Learning How to Let People In Without Disappearing

SYMPTOM: When Letting People In Feels Like Losing Yourself

After abandonment, trust does not feel like a virtue. It feels like a risk with a history. You want connection, but you no longer know how to enter it without bracing for loss. You remember the last time you trusted freely, how much of yourself you gave, how deeply you opened, and how quietly it all unraveled. So now, even when people seem safe, something inside you hesitates, not because you are unkind, but because you are cautious with what remains of you.

This symptom shows up when closeness feels confusing instead of comforting. When someone shows interest and your first instinct is not curiosity, but calculation. You wonder how much to share, how soon is too soon, and whether being honest will eventually cost you the relationship. You do not know how to trust without overextending, because in the past, trust required you to disappear.

Abandonment teaches you that trust means self-sacrifice. It convinces you that being chosen requires flexibility without limits, empathy without reciprocity, and patience without protection. So when you attempt to trust again, you either give too much too fast or hold back so tightly that intimacy never has a chance to form. You oscillate between overexposure and emotional distance, unsure how to find the middle ground.

This symptom is particularly painful because you *want* to trust. You are not closed to love. You are simply afraid of losing yourself again in the process. You remember how you once adjusted your needs to keep peace, how you silenced concerns to avoid conflict, and how you stayed longer than alignment allowed because trust felt like loyalty.

So now, even healthy connections feel unfamiliar. You are unsure how to remain yourself while letting someone close. You fear that trust will require compromise of identity, boundaries, or voice. And because no one taught you how to trust without abandoning yourself, you assume the two are inseparable.

You are not resistant to trust. You are resistant to self-erasure. This symptom keeps you stuck between longing and fear. You want connection, but you also want to remain intact. And until that tension is addressed, trust will always feel like a gamble instead of a choice.

TEACHING: Trust Is Not Losing Yourself; It Is Staying With Yourself While Opening the Door

Trust was never meant to require self-abandonment. It was designed to grow alongside self-awareness, not replace it. Healthy trust does not ask you to disappear; it asks you to remain present, honest, and anchored while allowing connection to unfold at a pace that honors truth.

One of the greatest misconceptions abandonment leaves behind is the belief that trust equals surrender. But trust is not submission to uncertainty. It is discernment practiced over time. It is allowing access gradually, not impulsively. It remains connected to your own needs while observing whether another person can meet you with consistency and care. 

God never calls you to trust blindly. He calls you to walk wisely. Trust that costs you your voice, your boundaries, or your sense of self is not biblical trust, it is fear-driven attachment. Scripture consistently emphasizes wisdom, counsel, and fruit over intensity or immediacy. Trust grows where safety is demonstrated, not where it is demanded.

Abandonment disrupts this process by making urgency feel necessary. It convinces you that if you do not attach quickly, you will lose the opportunity altogether. But healthy trust does not rush. It does not collapse your identity into another person's approval. It allows space for observation, communication, and mutual investment.

Trusting again does not mean returning to who you were before you were hurt. It means becoming someone who knows themselves better. Someone who recognizes early warning signs without becoming hypervigilant. Someone who can express needs without apologizing and walk away without self-blame if alignment is not present.

God does not ask you to trust people at the expense of yourself. He asks you to trust Him enough to remain honest, even when connection feels vulnerable. Trusting again is not about guaranteeing outcomes; it is about staying grounded regardless of outcome.

You are allowed to let people in slowly.
You are allowed to pause without withdrawing.
You are allowed to remain yourself while opening your heart.

Healing trust does not mean lowering your guard completely. It means replacing armor with boundaries and fear with awareness. It means trusting yourself first, your discernment, your limits, and your worth, so that trust with others becomes an extension of stability rather than a risk to it.

You do not heal abandonment by avoiding trust.
You heal it by redefining trust in a way that does not cost you your identity.

⚕ TRANSITION NOTE (Faith Clinic Continuity)

This chapter does not pressure you to trust faster.
It teaches you how to trust *truer*.
You are not broken because trust feels complicated.
You are healing because you refuse to disappear again.

☘ FAITH PRESCRIPTION

Rebuilding Trust While Staying Anchored in Yourself

Prescription Name: Anchored Trust Therapy
Dosage: Practiced intentionally in every emerging relationship
Duration: Ongoing; do not discontinue when vulnerability feels unfamiliar
Refills: Unlimited

Instructions for Use:

This prescription is not asking you to open yourself fully or immediately. It is asking you to remain connected to yourself while allowing others limited access. Trust does not begin with exposure; it begins with awareness. Healing trust requires you to stay present with your own needs, boundaries, and instincts while you observe whether someone can meet you with consistency and care.

You are instructed to release the belief that trust must be all or nothing. Healthy trust grows incrementally. It is built through repeated experiences of safety, not singular moments of vulnerability. Each interaction becomes information, not obligation.

When the urge arises to overextend, overshare, or overaccommodate to secure connection, pause and ask yourself: ***"Am I staying true to myself, or am I trying to secure belonging?"***

Trust that costs you your voice is not trust, it is self-abandonment. This prescription teaches you to remain grounded in your own values and limits while connection unfolds naturally.

Important Warning:
Avoid rushing trust to avoid loneliness. Loneliness addressed through self-erasure always returns.

🕊 HOLY SPIRIT CONSULT

Trusting Without Losing Your Center

The Holy Spirit is not urging you to trust recklessly.
He is inviting you to trust wisely.

He understands why you once disappeared to keep relationships intact. He knows how abandonment taught you to trade honesty for harmony. And without criticism, He is now restoring your center.

The Spirit is teaching you that trust begins with staying connected to yourself. That you are allowed to pause, ask questions, and observe patterns before offering deeper access. That trust is not proven by vulnerability alone, but by mutual consistency over time.

You are not being slow.
You are being intentional.
God is not asking you to hand yourself over. He is asking you to stay rooted while you open the door.

🙏 GUIDED PRAYER

(Steady. Honest. Grounded.)
God, I want to trust again, but I do not want to disappear in the process. I admit that in the past, trusting others cost me parts of myself. I adjusted, minimized, and silenced my needs because I was afraid of losing connection. I ask You now to help me trust in a new way.

Teach me how to remain anchored while letting people in.
Teach me how to speak honestly without fear of abandonment.

Teach me how to walk away without self-blame if alignment is not present.
I choose trust that does not require self-erasure.
I choose boundaries that protect connection instead of replacing it.
I trust You to guide me as I rebuild safely.
Amen.

📝 JOURNAL REFLECTION PAGE

Letting People In Without Leaving Yourself

Answer these questions slowly and without pressure.
1. What does self-abandonment look like for me in relationships?

____

____

____

____

2. What signals tell me I am starting to disappear?

____

____

____

____

3.   How do I usually overextend to feel chosen?

____

____

____

____

4.   What boundaries help me remain present with myself?

____

____

____

____

5.   What would trusting slowly look like in my life right now?

____

____

____

____

____

6.   What does it feel like to imagine staying fully myself while being close to others?

____

____

____

____

____

____

____

____

____

____

℞ CLOSING CLINICAL NOTE

This chapter does not demand that you trust faster.
It teaches you how to trust safer.
You are not broken because trust feels complicated.
You are healing because you refuse to disappear again.
Trust is not losing yourself.
It is staying with yourself, while allowing connection to grow.

PERSONAL NOTES

Chapter 13

"Discernment Without Fear"
How to Rebuild Wisdom Without Walls

SYMPTOM: When Caution Turns Into Constant Suspicion

After abandonment, discernment stops feeling like guidance and starts feeling like surveillance. You are always watching, analyzing, and preparing. You notice tone changes immediately. You track consistency closely. You read between lines that may or may not exist. You tell yourself you are simply being wise now, more alert than before, more spiritually mature.

But inside, you are tired.

This symptom shows up when your body remains tense even in safe situations. When your mind is constantly scanning for red flags instead of enjoying connection. When you struggle to relax because your nervous system believes vigilance is the only thing standing between you and another painful loss.

Abandonment trains discernment to over function. What was once intuition becomes anticipation. What was once wisdom becomes suspicion. You are no longer listening to the truth; you are listening for threat. And because fear is loud, it often overrides clarity.

You convince yourself that staying guarded is evidence of growth. You tell yourself that trusting less is the price of wisdom. You believe that walls are safer than boundaries because walls feel solid and immovable. But walls do not protect discernment, they isolate it.

This symptom often hides behind spiritual language. You call it being "led," "checking in your spirit," or "just being cautious." But fear-based discernment does not feel peaceful. It feels urgent. It feels tense. It feels like you must always stay alert or risk being blindsided again.

You are not paranoid. You are protecting yourself. But protection rooted in fear does not lead to wisdom. It leads to exhaustion. Abandonment teaches you that missing signs is dangerous, so you start seeing signs everywhere. You mistake neutrality for distance, pauses for rejection, and independence for abandonment. Over time, your discernment stops responding to reality and starts responding to memory.

You are not discerning the present. You are guarding against the past. And until this is addressed, fear will continue driving decisions in the name of wisdom.

TEACHING: Discernment Is Calm, Not Anxious

True discernment does not rush. It does not panic. It does not scan for danger constantly. Discernment rooted in God's wisdom is steady, observant, and grounded. It notices patterns over time instead of reacting to moments. It waits for clarity rather than forcing conclusions.

Fear-based discernment, on the other hand, demands certainty immediately. It cannot tolerate ambiguity. It pushes you to decide quickly, withdraw early, or shut down before risk has a chance to reveal itself. This is not wisdom. This is self-protection trying to stay in control.

Jesus modeled discernment without fear. He noticed people's hearts without bracing for betrayal. He allowed closeness without being naïve. He did not confuse awareness with avoidance. Even knowing He would be hurt, He did not harden Himself against connection.

Abandonment convinces you that safety comes from vigilance. God teaches that safety comes from trust, not blind trust in people, but grounded trust in Him and in the wisdom He grows within you over time. Discernment without fear allows space for observation. It gives relationships time to reveal their fruit. It does not need to preemptively withdraw to remain safe. It knows that truth surfaces naturally without being chased.

You do not need walls to be discerning. You need boundaries rooted in truth, not trauma. Fear-based discernment isolates you. It keeps you distant even from healthy connection. It prevents intimacy not because it is unsafe, but because it is unfamiliar. Wisdom, however, allows closeness while remaining anchored. It is not threatened by uncertainty because it trusts the process.

God does not call you to live suspicious. He calls you to live aware. Awareness watches without bracing. Wisdom listens without panicking. Discernment waits without withdrawing.

Rebuilding discernment after abandonment means learning how to trust your perception again without letting fear hijack it. It means allowing curiosity to replace suspicion. It means letting clarity emerge instead of forcing it.

You do not heal abandonment by seeing danger everywhere. You heal it by learning how to stay present long enough to see truth.

☤ CLINICAL NOTE (Faith Clinic Assessment)

Patient exhibits fear-driven discernment rooted in abandonment trauma.
Hypervigilance present; trust capacity restricted.
Treatment will focus on restoring calm-based wisdom and dismantling protective walls.

✪ FAITH PRESCRIPTION

Relearning Discernment Without Hypervigilance

Prescription Name: Calm Wisdom Therapy
Dosage: Applied relationally over time, not in moments of panic
Duration: Ongoing; do not discontinue during uncertainty
Refills: Unlimited

Instructions for Use:

This prescription retrains discernment to operate from calm rather than fear. You are instructed to notice the emotional tone behind your instincts. Wisdom feels grounded. Fear feels urgent. If urgency is driving the decision, pause.

Each time you feel compelled to withdraw quickly, ask yourself: **"What am I reacting to, present evidence or past pain?"**

Allow situations to unfold before assigning meaning. Discernment does not require immediate conclusions. It requires observation, consistency, and time.

Important Warning:
Avoid mistaking anxiety for intuition. Anxiety predicts loss; wisdom observes truth.

✧ HOLY SPIRIT CONSULT

Restoring Wisdom Without Walls

The Holy Spirit is not asking you to lower your standards. He is asking you to lower your defenses. He knows why you built walls. He honors your survival. But He is now inviting you to replace walls with boundaries, structures that protect without isolating.

The Spirit is teaching you that discernment grows in stillness, not suspicion. That clarity does not need panic to arrive. That fear does not get the final word in how you relate to others.

You are not losing wisdom by softening.
You are refining it.

🙏 GUIDED PRAYER

(Steady. Honest. Grounded.)
"God, I admit that fear has been speaking in the voice of discernment. I stayed guarded because I was hurt, not because I lacked wisdom. I ask You now to help me tell the difference between caution and fear, between awareness and anxiety.

Teach me how to discern calmly.
Teach me how to observe without bracing.
Teach me how to trust clarity to emerge without forcing it.
I release the need to stay hyper-alert.
I replace walls with boundaries.
I choose wisdom rooted in peace, not fear.
Amen."

📝 JOURNAL REFLECTION PAGE

Wisdom Without Walls
Answer slowly. Do not rush clarity.
1.   How does fear-based discernment feel in my body?

____

____

____

---

2. How does true wisdom feel different?

3. What situations trigger hypervigilance for me?

4. What walls have I built that now prevent connection?

____

____

____

5.   What would it look like to practice discernment with calm instead of control?

____

____

____

____

____

____

____

℞ CLOSING CLINICAL NOTE

This chapter does not strip you of wisdom.
It restores it.
You are not wrong for being cautious.
You are healing by learning how to be calm again.
Discernment does not require walls.
It requires truth, time, and peace.

Part 4

AFTERCARE

PERSONAL NOTES

Chapter 14

"When Old Wounds Get Triggered By New People"

Why Healing Doesn't Mean You'll Never React Again

SYMPTOM: When the Past Hijacks the Present Without Permission

One of the most discouraging moments in healing abandonment is the day you realize you reacted again. You thought you were past this. You thought you were healed enough. You had learned the language, done the work, set the boundaries, prayed the prayers. And then someone new says something familiar, delays a response, changes their tone, or pulls back slightly, and suddenly your chest tightens, your thoughts spiral, and your body reacts before your mind can intervene.

This symptom is not a failure of healing. It is a reminder of how deeply the wound once lived.

Old abandonment wounds do not announce themselves politely. They do not ask permission before surfacing. They respond reflexively to familiar sensations. Your body remembers what your mind has already processed. And when something in the present resembles something painful from the past, your nervous system reacts as if the past is happening again.

This symptom shows up when you feel embarrassed by your reaction. When you tell yourself you should know better by now. When you judge your progress because a familiar fear resurfaced. You feel frustrated because you thought healing meant you would never feel this way again.

Abandonment teaches your body to anticipate loss before it happens. So when new people unknowingly activate old memories, your system moves into protection mode. You may withdraw, overexplain, become hyper-alert, or emotionally shut down. Not because the present is unsafe, but because the past trained your body to respond quickly.

This is where many people shame themselves out of healing. They believe that reacting means regression. They assume that triggers invalidate progress. They tell themselves they are "back at square one," even when the reaction was shorter, milder, or more conscious than before.

You are not relapsing. You are encountering memories. Healing does not erase your history. It changes how you respond to it. But until your body fully relearns safety, old wounds may still speak when they recognize familiar patterns. That does not mean you are broken. It means your system is still learning how to stay present.

TEACHING: Triggers Are Invitations, Not Accusations

Triggers are not proof that you are unhealed. They are evidence that your system is still integrating safety. Healing is not the absence of reaction; it is the ability to recognize reaction without being ruled by it.

God does not shame you for being triggered. He does not interpret your reaction as disobedience or weakness. He understands that healing happens in layers and that the body often heals more slowly than the mind.

Jesus never rebuked people for reacting from pain. He responded with compassion, clarity, and truth. He did not demand instant transformation. He invited gradual restoration.

Abandonment convinces you that you must be flawless to be healed. It tells you that any reaction means you failed. But healing is not about perfection, it is about awareness. The moment you can say, "This is old pain speaking," you have already shifted out of survival mode.

Triggers reveal what still needs care, not condemnation. They show you where gentleness is required, where boundaries may need reinforcement, and where compassion toward yourself is necessary. They are not signals to retreat from connection, but invitations to stay present while tending to what surfaced.

New people are not responsible for old wounds. Old wounds are not evidence that new people are unsafe. The work is learning how to differentiate between the two.

God does not expect you to be untriggered. He invites you to be honest. Honest about what surfaced, why it surfaced, and what you need in that moment. Healing deepens when you stop punishing yourself for reactions and start responding with wisdom instead.

You do not move backward because something old spoke.
You move forward when you answer it with truth.

℞ CLINICAL NOTE (Faith Clinic Assessment)

The patient exhibits trauma memory activation in present relationships. Healing present; integration ongoing. Treatment will focus on trigger recognition without self-condemnation.

℞ FAITH PRESCRIPTION

Responding to Triggers Without Self-Shaming

Prescription Name: Trigger Awareness Integration Therapy
Dosage: Applied immediately when emotional activation occurs
Duration: Ongoing; do not discontinue after flare-ups
Refills: Unlimited

Instructions for Use:

This prescription trains you to pause instead of panic. When a trigger arises, you are instructed to name it without judgment. Say internally, "This feels familiar," instead of "Something is wrong with me."

Each time you feel activated, ask yourself: **"What is being remembered right now?"**

Triggers are not commands. They are messages. You are not required to act on them. You are only asked to listen long enough to respond wisely.

Important Warning:

Avoid turning awareness into self-interrogation. Understanding does not require self-punishment.

☙ HOLY SPIRIT CONSULT

Gentleness in the Middle of Reaction

The Holy Spirit does not withdraw when you are triggered. He draws closer. He understands that healing unfolds in layers. He knows your body learned survival before your mind learned truth. And He is not asking you to suppress reaction, He is teaching you how to remain present through it.

The Spirit is saying:
"You are not failing.
You are integrating.
Stay here. I am with you."

🙏 GUIDED PRAYER

(Compassionate. Stabilizing. Complete.)
"God, I felt something old rise again, and it scared me.

I thought I was past this, and when it surfaced, I felt disappointed in myself. I ask You now to help me respond with compassion instead of criticism.

Help me recognize memory without reliving it.
Help me stay present without shutting down.
Help me tend to what surfaced instead of running from it.
I release shame.
I release urgency.
I receive patience with myself.
I trust that healing is still happening—even here.
Amen."

📝 JOURNAL REFLECTION PAGE

Meeting Triggers With Truth

Answer honestly and gently.
1.   What specifically triggered me in this situation?

____

____

____

____

____

2.   What past experience did it remind me of?

____

____

____

____

____

____

____

3.   How did my body respond before my mind did?

____

____

____

____

____

4.   What did I need in that moment that I didn't give myself?

____

____

____

____

____

____

5.   How can I respond differently next time without self-blame?

____

____

____

____

____

____

____

____

⚕ CLOSING CLINICAL NOTE

This chapter does not accuse you of regression.
It honors your awareness.
Triggers are not setbacks.
They are checkpoints.
Healing is not about never reacting.
It is about learning how to stay when you do.

Chapter 15

"Love That Doesn't Require You To Shrink"

Redefining Connection After Abandonment

SYMPTOM: When You Mistake Shrinking For Compromise

After abandonment, love often feels conditional, even when no one explicitly says it is. You learn to read rooms carefully, adjust your tone strategically, and soften your needs preemptively. You tell yourself you are being flexible, understanding, and mature. But beneath the adaptability is a quiet fear: *If I am fully myself, I might be too much—and then I will be left again.*

This symptom shows up when you edit your emotions before sharing them. When you lower expectations so disappointment won't sting as much. When you accept less consistency, less clarity, and less effort because it feels safer than asking for more. You are not choosing unhealthy relationships; you are choosing survival strategies that once kept you connected.

Abandonment teaches you that love requires sacrifice and sacrifice slowly becomes self-reduction. You tell yourself that love means being patient, but patience turns into silence. You tell yourself that love means grace, but grace becomes self-neglect. You call it compromise, but compromise should never cost you your voice.

This symptom is reinforced by fear masquerading as humility. You convince yourself that wanting reciprocity is selfish, that expressing needs is demanding, and that staying small is spiritually admirable. But love that requires you to shrink is not love, it is tolerance wrapped in attachment.

You are not asking for too much. You are asking the wrong relationships to carry it. And until this pattern is named, you will continue confusing self-erasure with devotion and endurance with intimacy.

TEACHING: Love Expands You; It Does Not Reduce You

Healthy love does not require you to abandon yourself to be accepted. It invites your full presence. It allows difference without withdrawal. It honors needs without punishment. Love rooted in God's design is mutual, life-giving, and truth-centered. It does not grow by shrinking one person to maintain peace.

Jesus never asked people to disappear to remain connected. He invited them to bring their whole selves, questions, fears, needs, and all. Love, as modeled in Scripture, is not about managing someone else's comfort at the expense of your own integrity. It is about shared responsibility for care, communication, and growth.

Abandonment distorts this by teaching you that love is fragile and must be preserved through self-reduction. But love that cannot tolerate honesty is not fragile, it is incomplete. True connection does not punish authenticity. It responds to it.

God does not call you to love in ways that cost you your dignity. He does not equate suffering with holiness or silence with maturity. Love that reflects God's heart allows you to take up space without apology and to remain yourself without fear of consequence.

You are allowed to want clarity.
You are allowed to need consistency.
You are allowed to expect mutual effort.

Healing after abandonment means redefining love—not as endurance, but as expansion. Love should make you more yourself, not less. It should feel grounding, not destabilizing. It should not require you to dim your light to keep someone else comfortable.
You do not heal abandonment by learning how to shrink better.
You heal it by choosing love that can hold you fully.

⚕ CLINICAL NOTE (Faith Clinic Assessment)

Patient exhibits self-minimization patterns rooted in fear of abandonment. Attachment present; self-expression restricted. Treatment will focus on restoring relational equity and self-honor.

🔖 FAITH PRESCRIPTION

Practicing Love Without Self-Erasure

Prescription Name: Relational Expansion Therapy
Dosage: Applied consistently in all close relationships
Duration: Ongoing; do not discontinue when honesty feels risky
Refills: Unlimited

Instructions for Use:

This prescription invites you to notice where you shrink to maintain connection. Pay attention to moments when you silence yourself, soften your needs, or downplay your feelings to avoid conflict or withdrawal.
Each time you feel tempted to reduce yourself, pause and ask: **"What am I afraid will happen if I remain fully present?"**

Practice expressing needs calmly and clearly without apology. Allow relationships to respond to honesty rather than managing them through self-erasure.

Important Warning:
Avoid confusing peacekeeping with peace. Peacekeeping suppresses truth; peace sustains it.

🕊 HOLY SPIRIT CONSULT

Permission to Take Up Space

The Holy Spirit is not asking you to be smaller.
He is restoring your confidence to be whole.

He sees where you learned to disappear to stay connected. He understands how abandonment trained you to equate shrinking with safety. And He is now inviting you to step into love that can hold your full presence.

The Spirit is saying: "You do not have to diminish yourself to be loved. I created you to be known, not managed."

🙏 GUIDED PRAYER

(Affirming. Grounded. Whole.)
"God, I admit that I have shrunk myself to keep love. I softened my needs, silenced my voice, and called it compromise because I was afraid of being left again. I ask You now to heal the part of me that believes love requires self-erasure.

Teach me how to love without disappearing.
Teach me how to speak honestly without fear.
Teach me how to choose connection that allows me to remain whole.

I release the lie that being smaller makes me safer.
I choose love that expands me.
I choose relationships that can hold who I am.
Amen."

📝 JOURNAL REFLECTION PAGE

Choosing Expansion Over Shrinking
Answer gently and honestly.
1.   Where do I most often shrink in relationships?

____

____

____

____

____

____

____

2.   What needs do I silence to maintain peace?

____

____

____

____

____

3.   What fears surface when I imagine being fully myself?

____

____

____

____

____

____

4. How has shrinking protected me, and how has it harmed me?

____

____

____

____

____

5. What would love look like if I no longer had to disappear?

____

____

____

____

℞ CLOSING CLINICAL NOTE

This chapter does not accuse you of loving poorly.
It honors how much you tried to stay connected.
You are not difficult.
You are not demanding.
You are healing.
Love was never meant to cost you yourself.
It was meant to help you become whole.

PERSONAL NOTES

Chapter 16

"You're Allowed to Be Chosen And Cherished"

Undoing the Lie That Love Must Be Earned

SYMPTOM: When Being Wanted Feels Unfamiliar or Suspicious

One of the strangest side effects of abandonment is how uncomfortable genuine care can feel. When someone shows up consistently, communicates clearly, or chooses you without hesitation, something inside you tightens instead of relaxes. You look for the catch. You wait for the shift. You wonder what you are missing, because being chosen without effort does not match your internal blueprint for love.

This symptom shows up when affection feels overwhelming instead of reassuring. When consistency makes you anxious instead of calm. When being prioritized triggers suspicion rather than gratitude. You are not ungrateful, you are disoriented. Your nervous system learned love through unpredictability, so stability feels foreign.

Abandonment taught you that love is something you secure through effort. You learned to earn attention, negotiate consistency, and prove worth through endurance. So when love arrives without conditions, your body does not recognize it as safe. It feels undeserved, temporary, or too good to trust.

You may find yourself minimizing the care you receive. You downplay compliments. You deflect affection. You tell yourself not to get used to it. You stay emotionally braced, even in the presence of kindness, because history taught you that being chosen rarely lasts.

This symptom is painful because it keeps you from receiving what you have longed for. You finally encounter connection that does not require performance, and instead of resting, you retreat internally.

You are afraid that letting yourself enjoy being cherished will make the eventual loss unbearable.

You are not uncomfortable because love is wrong. You are uncomfortable because love without fear is new. And until this is named, you will continue mistaking unfamiliar safety for danger.

TEACHING: Being Chosen Is Not a Trap; It Is A Gift

God's design for love was never rooted in anxiety. From the beginning, love was meant to be chosen, not chased. Cherishing was meant to be mutual, not negotiated. Being wanted was not intended to trigger fear, it was meant to provide rest.

Abandonment distorts this by convincing you that love must be earned and maintained through vigilance. But Scripture consistently reveals a God who chooses first. Who loves without being convinced. Who cherishes without conditions. Divine love does not require audition; it extends invitation.

When God says you are chosen, He does not mean chosen because you performed well. He means chosen because He decided. That truth reshapes how you experience human connection. Healthy love mirrors this posture—not perfectly, but genuinely. It chooses without manipulation. It cherishes without withdrawal. It does not keep score.

Healing requires you to let go of the belief that being cherished makes you vulnerable to collapse. Yes, loss is possible. But withholding yourself from joy does not prevent pain; it only delays healing. You do not protect your heart by refusing to receive love. You protect it by staying grounded in truth while allowing connection to nourish you.

You are allowed to be chosen without earning it.
You are allowed to be cherished without proving sustainability.
You are allowed to receive love without bracing for loss.

God is not training you to tolerate affection cautiously. He is restoring your capacity to receive it fully. Cherishing does not make you weak; it reminds you that you were never meant to survive on scraps.

Being chosen does not mean you surrender discernment. It means you stop assuming abandonment is inevitable. It means you allow goodness to exist without immediately preparing for its disappearance. 

You do not dishonor your past by receiving love now.
You honor your healing by letting it in.

℞ CLINICAL NOTE (Faith Clinic Assessment)

Patient exhibits discomfort with consistent affection rooted in abandonment trauma. Receiving capacity restricted; self-bracing present. Treatment will focus on expanding tolerance for healthy attachment and care.

FAITH PRESCRIPTION

Learning to Receive Without Bracing

Prescription Name: Receiving Restoration Therapy
Dosage: Daily practice in moments of affection or consistency
Duration: Ongoing; do not discontinue when vulnerability increases
Refills: Unlimited

***Instructions for Use*:**

This prescription trains your nervous system to receive care without suspicion. When affection arises, you are instructed not to analyze it away. Pause. Breathe. Let the moment exist without preparing for its end.

Each time you feel the urge to deflect or minimize being chosen, ask yourself: *"**What would happen if I allowed this to be real right now?**"*

Receiving is not complacency. It is participation. You are not required to predict the future to enjoy the present. Healing happens when you stop treating love like a test you might fail.

Important Warning:
Avoid equating joy with naivety. Allowing yourself to be cherished is not ignorance, it is courage.

🕊 HOLY SPIRIT CONSULT

Permission to Rest in Being Chosen

The Holy Spirit is not rushing you into trust. He is inviting you into rest. He understands why you learned to brace. He honors the seasons where vigilance kept you safe. And now, gently, He is showing you that you do not have to stay guarded forever.

The Spirit is saying:
"You are not about to lose what I am restoring.
You are allowed to receive what you once survived without. God is not testing you with affection. He is healing you through it."

🙏 GUIDED PRAYER

(Receiving. Grounded. Gentle.)
God, I admit that being chosen still feels unfamiliar.
I have learned to earn love, manage connection, and brace for loss.
I ask You now to help me receive without fear.

Teach my heart that consistency is not a warning sign. Teach my body that affection does not require defense. Teach me how to rest in being wanted.

I release the need to stay guarded. I allow myself to be cherished. I trust that love can exist without collapse.

Amen.

📝 JOURNAL REFLECTION PAGE

Letting Yourself Be Chosen

Answer slowly and honestly.

1. How do I typically respond when someone chooses me clearly

____

____

____

____

____

2. What fears surface when I imagine being cherished long-term?

____

____

____

____

____

3.   How has bracing protected me, and how has it limited joy?

____

____

____

____

____

4.   What would it look like to receive love without shrinking or suspicion?

____

____

____

____

____

5.   What truth do I need to remind myself of when affection feels unfamiliar?

⚕ CLOSING CLINICAL NOTE

This chapter does not rush your healing. It widens your permission.
You are not foolish for wanting to be chosen.
You are not weak for enjoying being cherished.
You survived abandonment.
Now you are learning how to receive love without fear.

The Day You Stopped Asking What Was Wrong With You

There will come a quiet moment—long after you close this book—when something inside you finally exhales. Not because everything in your life is perfect, not because every relationship worked out, and not because abandonment never crosses your mind again. But because you stop asking the question that haunted you the longest: *What was wrong with me?*

That question was never the problem. Believing it deserved an answer was.
Abandonment has a way of turning pain into identity. It convinces you that being left means being lacking, that distance means deficiency, and that silence means you were somehow unworthy of

staying for. Over time, you didn't just experience abandonment, you internalized it. You adjusted your personality, your expectations, your needs, and your voice around the fear of being left again. You learned how to survive instead of how to receive.
And you did that brilliantly.

You adapted. You endured. You stayed strong when no one stayed with you. You figured things out without support. You carried emotional weight quietly. You learned to shrink, chase, numb, brace, and overthink, not because you were broken, but because you were trying to stay connected in a world that kept leaving.

This book was never about shaming those survival skills.  It was about retiring them. Because what protected you then is not meant to govern you now. Healing does not erase your story. It redeems your relationship with it. It teaches you how to look back without living there, remember without romanticizing, and move forward without dragging old wounds into new rooms. Healing is the moment you realize you don't need to understand every loss to stop carrying it.

You didn't lose because you weren't enough.
You lost because someone else couldn't stay.
That distinction changes everything.

The people who walked away did not take your worth with them. They took their capacity. They took their readiness. They took their consistency. And somewhere along the way, you accidentally picked up the responsibility for their absence and made it your burden to explain.

You can put that down now.
You are not behind.
You are not difficult.

You are not too much.
You are not hard to love.

You are healed enough to stop auditioning for connection and wise enough to stop chasing what God already released. You are grounded enough to trust again without disappearing, discerning enough to listen without fear, and whole enough to receive love without bracing for impact.

This is what freedom actually looks like, not the absence of pain, but the absence of self-betrayal. You will still feel things. You will still grieve some people. You will still have moments when old patterns knock on the door. But now, you recognize them. You don't confuse familiarity with fate. You don't confuse longing with alignment. You don't confuse effort with love. And you don't confuse being alone with being abandoned.

You know the difference now. The greatest miracle in this book is not that abandonment didn't happen. It's that abandonment no longer gets the final word. You were unseen for a season, but unseen was never a sentence.

You were overlooked, but never unloved.
You were left, but never lost.
And the life ahead of you will not require you to disappear to be chosen.

Close this book knowing this:

- ✓ You do not need to earn what is meant for you.
- ✓ You do not need to explain yourself to be worthy.
- ✓ You do not need closure to walk forward in peace.
- ✓ You are already chosen.
- ✓ You are already cherished.
- ✓ And you are finally free to live like it.

End of treatment.
Beginning of wholeness.

▨ FINAL DISCHARGE SUMMARY

Unseen Was a Season, Not a Sentence
You Were Never Unloved. You Were Being Prepared Out of Sight.

You did not imagine the pain.
You did not exaggerate the loss.
You were not "too much," "too sensitive," or "too attached."
You were abandoned.
And that truth matters, not so you can stay there, but so you can finally stop blaming yourself for what was never yours to carry.

This book was not written to convince you that abandonment didn't hurt. It was written to tell the truth about what it did to you, and to show you that its effects are not permanent, even if they felt defining.

Abandonment shaped your nervous system, your attachment patterns, your expectations, and the way you learned to survive connection. But it did not define your worth, your destiny, or your capacity for love.

For a long time, you lived unseen. Not unnoticed by God, but unchosen by people. Unprotected in places that should have been safe. Upheld in moments that required presence.

And because no one named it for you, you learned to normalize it. You learned to be strong instead of supported, adaptable instead of anchored, low maintenance instead of honest, independent instead of connected. You learned to chase clarity, shrink for peace, leave first to avoid being left, and brace for love instead of receiving it.

None of that made you broken.
It made you resourceful.
But survival is not the same as wholeness.
And coping is not the same as healing.

This clinic was not designed to make you tougher. It was designed to make you truer. To return you to yourself, not the version of you that learned how to endure abandonment quietly, but the version of you that knows how to remain present without disappearing, love without shrinking, trust without erasing yourself, and receive without bracing for loss.

You were never unloved.
You were just loved inconsistently.
And inconsistency leaves scars that look like self-doubt, hypervigilance, emotional exhaustion, and a quiet fear that says, *"Don't get too comfortable, this won't last."*

But here is what must be said clearly, finally, and without spiritual bypassing:

- ✓ God did not abandon you.
- ✓ He did not overlook you.
- ✓ He did not delay love as punishment or test your worth through absence.
- ✓ You were unseen by people, but you were being formed out of sight.
- ✓ Unseen seasons are not evidence of rejection.
  They are spaces of preparation.
- ✓ Roots grow underground before anything blooms.
- ✓ Healing often happens quietly before it ever becomes visible.
- ✓ And restoration usually looks lonely before it looks like love.
- ✓ You were not being ignored.
- ✓ You were being fortified.

This discharge does not mean your life will now be free of loss, disappointment, or relational risk. It means you are no longer living from abandonment as your reference point. It means you are no longer chasing what God has already released, shrinking to be tolerated, or mistaking familiarity for alignment.

You now know the difference between longing and love.
Between discernment and fear.
Between trust and self-erasure.
Between peace and numbness.
Between being chosen and trying to earn belonging.
You are being released, not because you are "fixed," but because you are *aware*.
Aware enough to notice when you are disappearing.
Aware enough to stop chasing.
Aware enough to choose yourself without guilt.
Aware enough to receive love without panic.
This is not the end of your healing.
It is the end of your self-abandonment.
You are no longer required to prove you are worth staying for.
You are no longer obligated to explain your pain to be believed.
You are no longer waiting for closure to move forward.
You are allowed to be chosen.
You are allowed to be cherished.
You are allowed to take up space.
You are allowed to rest.
And most importantly:
You are allowed to trust that what is meant for you will meet you without pursuit.

⚕ OFFICIAL DISCHARGE STATUS

Diagnosis:
Abandonment trauma with adaptive survival responses
Treatment Completed:
✓ Truth-based awareness

DR. PATRICIA S. TANNER

✓ Emotional re-regulation
✓ Identity restoration
✓ Relational recalibration
✓ Permission to receive

Aftercare Instructions:
Continue choosing alignment over attachment.
Continue honoring your boundaries without apology.
Continue allowing love to be gentle, mutual, and real.

Emergency Reminder:
If you feel the urge to chase, shrink, or disappear—pause.
That is not intuition. That is an old wound asking for reassurance,
not obedience.

✍ FINAL WORD TO THE READER

You were not forgotten.
You were not passed over.
You were not late.
You were becoming.
And now, you are free to live from that truth—
whole, present, and no longer asking the past to explain itself.
Discharge complete.
Go live like someone who knows they were never unloved.

⚕ DOCTOR'S ORDERS

Because Healing Needs Structure (Not Vibes)
Patient Name: You
Diagnosis: Abandonment Recovery: In Active Healing Phase
Attending Physician: Faith Clinic
Status: Stable, Growing, No Longer Self-Abandoning

PRIMARY TREATMENT GOAL

Restore peace, dignity, and relational health without shrinking, chasing, numbing, or overexplaining. This care plan is not optional comfort; it is **necessary structure** for sustained healing.

📋 DAILY ORDERS (DO NOT SKIP)

1. Take One Dose of Truth Every Morning
Before checking messages, emails, or memories, remind yourself:
I do not need to be chosen today to be worthy. I already am.
Truth must be taken **before** exposure to triggers.

2. Practice Presence Over Prediction
You are ordered to stop forecasting endings.
No reading between lines.
No rehearsing future loss.
If the thought begins with *"What if they…"* it is **not** wisdom.
Redirect immediately.

3. Maintain Emotional Boundaries
You are no longer permitted to:
- Overexplain your needs
- Justify your boundaries
- Apologize for being honest

Boundaries are **not debates**. They are information.

4. Eat Real Rest (Not Emotional Fasting)
Rest is prescribed daily.
This includes:
- Silence without guilt
- Joy without bracing
- Stillness without productivity

You are not lazy.
You are healing.

🚫 STRICTLY PROHIBITED ACTIVITIES

Effective immediately, patient must avoid the following behaviors:
- ✘ Chasing clarity from unavailable people
- ✘ Shrinking to keep peace
- ✘ Romanticizing inconsistency
- ✘ Using closure as an excuse to stay stuck
- ✘ Calling anxiety "discernment"
- ✘ Reopening wounds to prove you're healed

Noncompliance will result in emotional relapse.

🧠 WEEKLY CHECKPOINTS

Once per week, patient must review the following:
- Where did I stay present instead of self-abandoning?
- Where did I choose peace instead of pursuit?
- Where did I honor truth instead of familiarity?
- Where did I receive love without bracing?

Progress is measured by **awareness**, not perfection.

✊ EMERGENCY PROTOCOL (USE AS NEEDED)

If patient experiences sudden urges to:
- Chase
- Shrink
- Overfunction
- Leave first
- Numb out
-

Immediate Response Required:
1. Pause. Breathe. Ground.
2. Name the trigger without shame.
3. Ask: *Is this old pain or present truth?*
4. Choose the response that preserves dignity.

If confusion persists, return to **stillness**, not action.

LONG-TERM CARE INSTRUCTIONS

Healing is not linear.
Triggers do not cancel progress.
Loneliness does not mean abandonment returned.

Patient is cleared to:
- Trust again without disappearing
- Love again without self-erasure
- Rest again without fear
- Be chosen without earning

PHYSICIAN'S FINAL NOTE

You are no longer required to survive your life.
You are now authorized to **live it**.
Structure does not restrict healing.

It **protects** it.
Follow orders.
Protect your peace.
Recovery is in progress.

PERSONAL NOTES

ABOUT THE AUTHOR

Dr. Patricia Tanner was born and raised in Sanford FL. She comes from a family of three siblings. Patricia Tanner is the founder of Multhai International Realty, Multhai Asset Management Services, and Multhai Investment Group which is located in Sanford, Florida. She is a graduate of the University of Central Florida, where she received a Bachelor of Science in Business Administration and a minor in Human Resources Management.

Dr. Tanner began her career shortly thereafter as a Regional Property Manager in the apartment community. Throughout her career in property management, she has built interpersonal relationships with corporate clients. She has a successful track record of increasing company revenues over $5 million annually, through hard work, commitment, creativeness, and strategic planning.

Her experience and leadership role eventually led her to achieve a Florida Real Estate Broker license. She spent fifteen years in the Real Estate field while completing a Master of Arts in Human Resources Management from Webster University, and a Master of Public Administration from Troy University. It was in this capacity that she decided to open her own brokerage company, Multhai International Realty.

In addition, Dr. Tanner finds time in her busy schedule to participate in her own Non-For-Profit Organization, Stones 2 Homes. She remains President of her organization in which she helps people build, keep, or purchase homes in affordable communities. She is the founder of PNT Property Partners in which she buys vacant land, develops it, and constructs brand new construction homes in Sanford Florida. Her overall goal is to educate and provide resources to help people overcome financial hardships and credit disadvantage to live the American Dream through homeownership in spite of economic hardship. Through her visions she will continue to grow as an entrepreneur and is willing to share her knowledge, experience, and expertise with anyone who is willing to learn.

MORE BOOKS BY THE AUTHOR

Welcome to the Faith Clinic—where your soul doesn't need to be perfect to be healed.

You've smiled through burnout. Quoted scripture while quietly unraveling. Prayed, fasted, and still felt like your faith flatlined. If that's you, Faith Clinic: Volume I is your spiritual prescription.

Dr. Patricia S. Tanner—known as The Faith Doctor—invites you into a raw, grace-filled recovery journey for the soul. With 7 powerful doses of faith-infused wisdom, this book delivers healing where performance failed and offers truth where church hurt left a scar. Designed especially for spiritually exhausted youth and young adults, each "dose" reads like an IV drip of hope for believers secretly running on empty.

You don't need to be okay to show up. You just need to be willing. The clinic is open.

NOW AVAILABLE:

www.amazon.com

Healing was just the beginning. Now it's time to grow.

If Faith Clinic Volume I met you in crisis, Volume II meets you in recovery. Because faith isn't a one-time fix—it's a lifestyle that needs maintenance, accountability, and consistency. Welcome to your follow-up care plan.

In Faith Clinic: Volume II, Dr. Patricia S. Tanner—aka The Faith Doctor—guides you through the next level of your spiritual healing journey. From navigating church trauma and burnout to facing silence from God and rediscovering purpose, this book goes deeper than devotionals. It's not about hype—it's about habits that sustain real, lasting transformation.

With raw wisdom, relatable stories, and no-shame truths, each chapter is a spiritual check-in for believers who want to thrive—not just survive. Whether you're wrestling with doubt, craving stability, or simply ready to grow up in God, this clinic is for you.

You've detoxed. Now it's time to build. Let's get you discharge-ready.

NOW AVAILABLE:
www.amazon.com

Welcome to the Faith Clinic: Anxiety Edition — where God doesn't coddle your coping mechanisms but confronts them with surgical precision.

This book is for the ones who love Jesus but still can't sleep. For the worship leaders crying in church bathrooms. For the believers who pray in spirals, fight shame on Sundays, and secretly think, "Maybe I'm the only one who can't seem to breathe through this." You're not crazy. You're just in a fight — and this book is your spiritual triage.

Inside you'll find:
- ☑ Panic attacks in pews and the prayers that still work.
- ☑ Scriptures that talk you off the ledge.
- ☑ What to do when you feel numb and God feels quiet.
- ☑ How to walk out of shame loops, judgment spirals, and performance religion.

This isn't just encouragement. It's equipment.
Because healing isn't a moment — it's a walk.

NOW AVAILABLE:

www.amazon.com

Welcome to the Faith Clinic: Stress Edition — where we don't hand you cute verses and clichés. We hand you spiritual prescriptions for real pressure, real panic, and real prayers from tired believers holding it together by a thread.

This book is for the overwhelmed—those trusting God while juggling bills, burnout, hustle culture, and holy frustration. If you've ever whispered, "God, are You even watching this mess?" this is for you.

Inside you'll find raw, soul-hitting chapters like:

- "God, I Trust You — But These Bills Keep Coming"

- "If Rest Is Holy, Why Does It Feel Like Slacking?"

- "I'm Tired of Smiling So You Won't Worry"

This isn't fluff. It's real talk for real stress—and a reminder that you're not forgotten, you're being fortified.

The Faith Clinic is open. Breathe in & take your spiritual vitamins. Healing begins here.

NOW AVAILABLE:
www.amazon.com

This isn't just a feeling — it's a flare signal from the soul. You pray, serve, and believe in God, but something deep inside is still simmering. Welcome to the Faith Clinic: Anger Edition — where suppressed emotions meet sacred intervention.

In this volume, Dr. Patricia S. Tanner guides you through spiritual triage for:

- ☑ Silent rage and emotional suppression

- ☑ The grief–anger connection

- ☑ Rejection wounds from childhood to church hurt

This isn't a lecture. It's a spiritual detox. No shame. No sugar-coating. Just raw, honest healing. Whether you're snapping at loved ones or silently seething under the surface, this book meets you at the boiling point—and leads you to the breakthrough.

🩺 This is the clinic.

🩸 This is your moment.

And God is ready to heal the anger behind your amen.

NOW AVAILABLE:

www.amazon.com

30 Days Of Grieving

Given By The Inspiration Of God

Healing From COVID-19

Almost a year later, it hit me... My mother was gone, and I was still stuck at the hospital. I had tried everything from crying to counseling, and even prayer. Pray they told me. Trust God they insisted. But it seemed as if nothing was working. I was hurt, dealing with my reality: my mother was not coming back.

While journeying through grief, it was under the divine 'Inspiration of God' that He placed me in a trance. While I was gaining a revelation about grief, He gave me this journal, '30 Days Of Grieving.'

NOW AVAILABLE:

www.amazon.com

Can Salvation Get You Into Heaven? The Answer Is Yes! offers a powerful and biblically grounded exploration of God's eternal plan, revealing the heart of the Gospel and the assurance of salvation through Jesus Christ.

 Unpacking life's most vital questions—Who is God? Why were we created? What does Jesus' life mean for us?—this book brings clarity to the believer's journey and confirms that salvation, once received, is eternally secure.

Whether you're seeking understanding or affirming your faith, this inspiring guide will lead you into the confidence and joy of knowing heaven is your eternal home.

NOW AVAILABLE:
www.amazon.com

DR. PATRICIA S. TANNER

The Bench That Waited is a bold and prophetic call to action for believers who've grown comfortable in church attendance but stagnant in purpose.

With raw honesty and spiritual insight, Patricia Tanner exposes the quiet crisis of passive faith—where callings are delayed and obedience is optional.

Through Scripture, stories, and reflection, this book urges readers to rise from routine, break free from spiritual stagnation, and step boldly into their Kingdom assignment. The bench has waited long enough—will you?

NOW AVAILABLE:
www.amazon.com

What happens when the Kingdom becomes a stranger?

The Godless Climb is not a rejection of faith—it is a raw, unflinching journey through what remains when belief unravels. With brutal honesty and tender grace, this book explores the spiritual free fall that follows the loss of divine certainty, the ache of unanswered prayers, and the void left when God no longer feels near.

Written for those who have quietly slipped out of the pews and into a wilderness of doubt, grief, and inner searching, this is not a triumph story—but a survival story. A confession. A sacred wrestle. Through personal reflection and prophetic insight, the author unpacks what it means to climb without a safety net, to live without the scaffolding of religious performance, and to build a new compass in the absence of old crutches.

You haven't arrived. But you're still climbing. And that is holy.

NOW AVAILABLE:

www.amazon.com

It Was The God In

Me

Success can be attributed to many things. Depending on the person who has obtained success would determine those to whom they attribute their success. Some give credit to their daily routine while others give credit to a mentor or some sort of system they followed. When I think about my success, the only person who I can give the credit to is God.

In this memoir, I share the successes and failures I have experienced throughout my life. From my individual experiences to my entrepreneurial journey, I share how God has walked with me every step of the way.

Come and see.. It Was The God In Me!!

NOW AVAILABLE:

www.amazon.com

The Triple 7 Formula is designed for business owners who are looking forward to hitting the million-dollar mark in their business. If you own a business and seem to be running in financial circles, this book will get you on track to simultaneously gaining sound business structure and millions in your bank account.

It was through many conversations with business owners lacking financial gain that prompted Patricia to share her blueprint for millionaire status. Through this book, she demonstrates how to gain financial ground by developing strong teams, implementing systems, and setting stackable goals. If you are ready to gain a laser sharp focus, and implement these clear steps, you will position yourself for financial greatness. Your business will be sound, and you will see financial growth beyond your wildest dreams!!

NOW AVAILABLE:

www.amazon.com

The Triple 7 Formula is specifically crafted for business owners aspiring to reach the million-dollar milestone. If you are a business owner feeling stuck in financial cycles, this book will set you on the path to building both a solid business structure and financial success.

This workbook is designed to complement the textbook of the same name. As you progress through its pages, you will be inspired to take decisive steps toward becoming a millionaire. From constructing your business framework to creating the millionaire's avatar, this process will expand your knowledge and mindset. Not only will you chart a course to financial success, but you will also identify your accountability circle and select a mentor to guide you toward greatness.

I cannot guarantee millionaire status unless you actively follow the steps to begin your journey. If you are searching for a get rich quick scheme, this workbook is not for you. I am looking for those ready to put in the effort—and since you are reading this, I believe that's you!

You have finally found it: Your roadmap to millions!

NOW AVAILABLE:
WWW.Amazon.com

Find Patricia on The Web:

www.PatriciaTanner.com

Follow Patricia on social media:

Facebook & Instagram: @PatriciaTannerInc

DR. PATRICIA S. TANNER